LNER 4-6-0s
A PICTORIAL TRIBUTE

Peter Swinger

Ian Allan
60th
ANNIVERSARY

Above:
Class B12 No 8540 as originally built by the Great Eastern Railway at Stratford in July 1917, with Belpaire firebox. The engine is waiting to leave Ipswich with a train for London; whilst the date is lost, the photograph must have been taken early in LNER days, for the number is still carried upon the tender beneath small lettering denoting ownership. *Author's collection*

CONTENTS

First published 2002

ISBN 0 7110 2808 7

Published by Ian Allan Publishing

an imprint of Ian Allan Publishing Ltd, Hersham, Surrey KT12 4RG.
Printed by Ian Allan Printing Ltd, Hersham, Surrey KT12 4RG.

Code: 0205/B1

INTRODUCTION

Following the Grouping of the railways of Great Britain in 1923 and the consequent creation of the London & North Eastern Railway, the directors of the new company decided upon a classification system of its locomotives which was simple and served the railway well throughout its lifetime. Pacifics were to be classified 'A', 4-6-0s 'B', Atlantics 'C' and so on through the alphabet, this system being retained post-Nationalisation.

The 4-6-0 classes of the LNER were thus classified from B1 to B19 but there were only 17 classes in all, and of these but two were of LNER origin (with a later rebuild of one of those), the balance being inherited from the constituent companies. Of those constituents, the largest, the Great Northern Railway, had eschewed the 4-6-0 wheel arrangement, preferring to rely upon Atlantics for its express and other main-line passenger duties, and Moguls for fast freight work. However, the Great Central Railway and the North Eastern Railway used the 4-6-0 wheel arrangement extensively. At the Grouping the LNER inherited a total of 263 4-6-0s from the Great Central Railway, the North Eastern Railway

and the Great Eastern Railway; of these, 90 came from the Great Central, spread over nine classes, 103 from four North Eastern classes and 70 from a single class of Great Eastern engine. This number rose to 305 in 1924 with additions of GCR and NER designs which were already in production at the Grouping. Although they never all existed together, the number of LNER 4-6-0s finally totalled 798, but some of them were built in British Railways days, the maximum number ever in traffic at one time being 610.

The preservation movement has not been kind to the LNER, and particularly not in respect of its 4-6-0s; just three locomotives have survived. One 'B12' is still with us (its home nominally on the North Norfolk Railway, but it is a nomadic beast), as are two of Edward Thompson's 'B1s', although one of the latter was actually turned out after Nationalisation.

Consideration was given to dealing with the locomotives in LNER class-number sequence, but as changes to class numbering occurred under the LNER this course of action might have caused confusion; instead they are dealt with geographically and chronologically, starting in East Anglia and working northwards through LNER territory, with the engines of LNER design and construction appearing at the end of the book.

Above:
Class B12/1 No 61563 at Inverurie Works in October 1950, in lined BR black but coupled to a tender in apple green with 'BRITISH RAILWAYS' lettering.
T. B. Owen/Colour-Rail (SC383)

Above:
Just look what can happen to Brunswick green! Class B17/6 No 61658 *The Essex Regiment* is nearly black at Colchester shed in October 1958 — a reflection of the lowering storm clouds, or is the engine simply filthy? *D. T. Cobbe collection/Colour-Rail (BRE361)*

CLASS SUMMARY

London & North Eastern Railway 4-6-0s

Class B1 (later B18)
Robinson 6ft 9in Class 8C engine for the
Great Central Railway introduced in 1903,
two locomotives built — reclassified Class B18 in 1943

Class B2 (later B19)
Robinson 6ft 9in Class 1 engine for the
Great Central Railway introduced in 1912,
six locomotives built — reclassified Class B19 in 1945

Class B3
Robinson 6ft 9in Class 9P engine for the
Great Central Railway introduced in 1917,
six locomotives built

Class B4
Robinson 6ft 7in Class 8F engine for the
Great Central Railway introduced in 1906,
10 locomotives built

Class B5
Robinson 6ft 1in Class 8 engine for the
Great Central Railway introduced in 1902,
14 locomotives built

Class B6
Robinson 5ft 8in Class 8N engine for the
Great Central Railway introduced in 1918,
three locomotives built

Class B7
Robinson 5ft 8in Class 9Q engine for the
Great Central Railway introduced in 1921,
28 locomotives built and a further 10 after Grouping

Class B8
Robinson 5ft 7in Class 1A engine for the
Great Central Railway introduced in 1913,
11 locomotives built

Class B9
Robinson 5ft 4in Class 8G engine for the
Great Central Railway introduced in 1906,
10 locomotives built

Class B12
Holden 6ft 6in Class S69 engine for the
Great Eastern Railway introduced in 1911,
70 locomotives built and a further 10 after Grouping

Class B13
Worsdell 6ft 1¼in Class S engine for the
North Eastern Railway introduced in 1899,
40 locomotives built

Class B14
Worsdell 6ft 8¼ in Class S1 engine for the
North Eastern Railway introduced in 1900,
five locomotives built

Class B15
Raven 6ft 1¼in Class S2 engine for the
North Eastern Railway introduced in 1911,
20 locomotives built

Above:
Class B12 No 8528 with a rake of GER stock in
LNER days. *Author's collection*

Class B16
Raven 5ft 8in Class S3 engine for the
North Eastern Railway introduced in 1919,
38 locomotives built and a further 32 after
Grouping

Class B17
Gresley 6ft 8in engine for the London &
North Eastern Railway introduced in 1928,
73 locomotives built

Class B1
Thompson 6ft 2in engine for the London &
North Eastern Railway introduced in 1942,
274 locomotives built and a further 136 after
Nationalisation

Class B2
Thompson rebuilds from Gresley Class B17

Principal dimensions of LNER 4-6-0s in classification sequence at the Grouping and subsequently for classes built by the LNER

Class	Builder	Bogie dia	Driving dia	Length	Boiler dia	Cylinders
B1	LNER	3ft 2in	6ft 2in	61ft 7in	5ft 6in	2 (O) — 20x26in
B2	LNER	3ft 2in	6ft 8in	61ft 9in *	5ft 6in	2 (O) — 20x26in
B3	GCR	3ft 6in	6ft 9in	63ft	5ft 6in	4 — 16x26in
B4	GCR	3ft 6in	6ft 7in	61ft 11in	5ft	2 (O) — 19x26in
B5	GCR	3ft 6in	6ft 1in	60ft 9in	4ft 9in	2 (O) — 19x26in
B6	GCR	3ft 6in	5ft 8in	61ft 2in	5ft 6in	2 (O) — 21x26in
B7	GCR	3ft 6in	5ft 8in	63ft	5ft 6in	4 — 16x26in
B8	GCR	3ft 6in	5ft 7in	63ft	5ft 6in	2 (I) — 21½x26in
B9	GCR	3ft 6in	5ft 4in	60ft 9in	5ft	2 (O) — 19x26in
B12	GER	3ft 3in	6ft 6in	57ft 7in	5ft 1⅛in	2 (I) — 20x28in
B13	NER	3ft 7¾in	6ft 1¼in	61ft ¾in	4ft 9in	2 (O) — 20x26in
B14	NER	3ft 7¾in	6ft 8¼in	61ft 11in	4ft 9 in	2 (O) — 20x26in
B15	NER	3ft 7¾in	6ft 1¼in	61ft ¾in	5ft 6in	2 (O) — 20x26in
B16	NER	3ft 1in	6ft 8in	62ft 6in	5ft 6in	3 — 18½x26in
B17/1	LNER	3ft 2in	6ft 8in	58ft 4in	5ft 6in	3 — 17½x26in
B17/5					62ft 9in	
B17/6					62ft 2in	
B18	GCR	3ft 6in	6ft 9in	61ft 11¼in	5ft	2 (O) — 21x26in (No 5195)
						2 (O) — 19x26in (No 5196)
B19	GCR	3ft 6in	6ft 9in	63ft	5ft 6in	2 (I) — 20x26in (Nos 423/4/7)
						2 (I) — 21½x26in (Nos 425/6/8)

* with ex-NER tender; 62ft 2in with Group Standard tender, 62ft 1in with ex-'P1' tender

Holden Class S69 — LNER Class B12
6ft 6in engines

The sole example of the 4-6-0 wheel arrangement to be employed by the Great Eastern Railway was Stratford's *magnum opus*, purely the work of the Stratford Design Office though nominally credited to Stephen Dewar Holden. Increasing train loads on the Great Eastern in the first decade of the 20th century meant that the worthy and sturdy 7ft 'Claud Hamilton' 4-4-0s were beginning to find life a little hard, and greater power was called for. The major problem was to provide that greater power within the restrictions imposed by the Civil Engineer and a restriction in length imposed by the plethora of 50ft turntables which abounded within Great Eastern territory.

As early as July 1908 an order was issued for the preparation of drawings for a new six-coupled express passenger locomotive, but construction was not authorised until January 1911. The 7ft driving wheel had become something of a Holy Grail on Stratford passenger engines but was sacrificed in favour of 6ft 6in on the new locomotive which was classified S69. Inside cylinders were, however, retained (making life that much more difficult for the maintenance staff), though enlarged from the 19x26in of the 'Claud' to 20x28in. The very large cab, in conjunction with the short standard Great Eastern tender, gave the new engine an appearance of being larger than it actually was. The wheelbase was 48ft 3in and it had a singularly low axle-loading of 15 tons 13cwt. The boiler was extended in all dimensions over that of the 'Claud Hamilton' 4-4-0, and the front of the Belpaire firebox was over the centre coupled axle; it retained the polished-steel ring on the smokebox and had elegant cut-out valances over the top half of the driving wheels beneath the footplating.

On 31 December 1911 the first 'S69' 4-6-0 made its trial run from Stratford Works — nearly a year after construction had been authorised. By 1921 a total of 71 'S69s' had been built, numbered 1500 to 1570, but one of them had the misfortune to enjoy possibly the shortest working life of any steam locomotive. No 1506 left Stratford Works in February

Right:
One of the experiments that the LNER wrought upon the 'B12' was the fitting of ACFI water-feed equipment, which served to render an elegant locomotive rather hideous or, as someone wrote, 'like a Victorian lady with the skirts about her ears'. In 1938 No 8532 was seen so equipped on Southend ashpits in fully lined apple-green livery with shaded lettering, and still with Belpaire boiler and the intricate fretworking over the driving wheels.
Colour-Rail (NE11)

1913 but was in collision with 2-4-0 No 471 at the London end of Colchester station on 12 July that same year whilst working a Cromer–London express and was damaged beyond economic repair. The running-number was not reused, the replacement engine being No 1535. Nos 1500-40 were built in batches by Stratford up until 1917; then an order was placed with W. Beardmore & Co of Glasgow for 20 more, which were delivered in 1920/1, numbered 1541-60. Stratford built the final pre-Grouping batch of 10 in 1920, numbered 1561-70.

Following the Grouping the GER 'S69' became LNER Class B12, and the first post-Grouping construction of the class took place in 1928, when Beyer, Peacock & Co built 10. These engines differed from the original 71 (which were always referred to as 'B12GE' in the engine-diagram book) in that the smokebox was extended by 9in, a new pattern of cast-iron chimney was fitted and the main frames were deepened between the cylinders and the driving axle. The main visual difference was the abandonment of the decorative valances, which made a dramatic difference to the appearance of the engines. This variation took the classification 'B12/2', and the various changes added 2 tons 19cwt to the weight of the engines, the maximum axle load being increased to 15 tons 17cwt.

Continuing improvements to the permanent way on the Great Eastern section of the LNER meant that by 1931 it was possible to increase the weight of the 'B12s', which, at last, allowed for more extensive rebuilding of the class. The work was carried out at Stratford under the direction of Edward Thompson, who was Assistant Mechanical Engineer to Gresley at that works. The rebuilds were classified 'B12/3' and were 2in longer than the originals due to the fitting of Group Standard buffers which were longer than the Great Eastern variety. They were dramatically different in appearance, due to the fact that the new boilers of Gresley design were 5ft 6in in diameter and were round-topped, and the valances were removed from the GE-built engines. Somewhat surprisingly, right-hand drive was retained, and the adhesive weight was increased from 43 tons 8cwt to 48 tons 2cwt, but the original cylinder size and boiler pressure were retained, the tractive effort remaining unchanged at 21,969lb at 85% cut-off. The maximum axle-load went up to exactly 17 tons.

During World War 2 a number of 'B12/3s' were used on ambulance trains which took them into other companies' territories. In order to accommodate this work the cab footsteps were cut back and toe apertures cut into the backing plate to the steps. As the 'B17' class became more widely available and 'B12s' were released by the Great Eastern section, a number of them were moved north of the border to work on the Great North of Scotland section. Similar rebuilding to that carried out on the 'B12/3s' was not possible on these locomotives, due to the maximum permitted axle load on the GNS section. When further replacement boilers were required in 1941 the opportunity was taken to redesign the existing boilers to current LNER standards; they were rebuilt with round-top instead of Belpaire fireboxes and the decorative valances disappeared; late in 1948 this variation was designated 'B12/4'. The entire class was equipped with Great Eastern-pattern tenders, and, whilst there were differences in coal and water capacity, in appearance they were virtually identical.

Right:
No 8579 was built for the LNER by Beyer, Peacock & Co under Works No 6495 in September 1928 as the penultimate member of the 'B12' class and was rebuilt in May 1932. This picture was taken at Ipswich on 19 July that year, and shows how a 'B12' looked in LNER days without a Belpaire firebox or the cut-outs over the driving wheels. By this time, 'LNER' was in larger lettering upon the tender and the locomotive's number had moved to the cab sides.
Author's collection

Above:
Class B12/1 No 61507 poses on the turntable at Kittybrewster, Aberdeen, on Wednesday 22 August 1951; it is still in apple green but has received 'BRITISH RAILWAYS' lettering on its tender. *Roger Harrison*

Right:
No 61539 at Aberdeen, on Thursday 14 August 1952. There are some interesting points about the livery: the early BR emblem is extremely small on the tender, and the lining around the cab-side number is an oblong, whereas it was usual practice to allow the lining to follow the line of the footplating. The locomotive retains its Belpaire firebox.
Roger Harrison

Numbering

The first five members of the class were built in 1911 and 1912 numbered 1500-4; because of the running-number assigned to the first 'B12' they were always known to enginemen as '1500s'. The year 1913 saw a further 15 examples built in two batches at Stratford, numbered 1505-19, whilst Nos 1520-9 came in 1914, followed by 1530-5 later that year and in 1915. Five were built from 1915 to 1917, numbered 1536-40, then there was a break until 1920, when W. Beardmore & Co built Nos 1541-60 whilst Stratford simultaneously constructed Nos 1561-70. No further 'B12s' were built by the GER, but in 1928 Beyer, Peacock & Co built 10, numbered 8571-80 for the LNER, which had added 7,000 to the Great Eastern numbers. These 80 locomotives were allocated numbers 7415-94 under the 1942 renumbering scheme, with the intention of clearing GE-section numbers from 8301 for the construction of the Thompson 'B1' class. When just 11 of the class had been so treated (Nos 7426/37/49/67/70/2/6/9/82/8/91) the scheme was abandoned, although the engines ran with their new numbers until 1943. Under the 1946 renumbering scheme the 'B12s' reverted to 1500-80, and from 1948, under British Railways, 60,000 was added.

Liveries

The first batch of 'B12s' to emerge from Stratford Works were finished in the glorious Great Eastern Railway passenger-locomotive livery of royal blue with scarlet lining and vermilion buffer-beams and side-rods, augmented with brass beading on the splashers and the steel ring on the smokebox which had become such a part of Great Eastern passenger locomotives. Following the outbreak of World War 1, that glorious livery (would that colour photography had come along much earlier!) was abandoned, and the Great Eastern Railway turned its locomotives out in a drab pale grey; the 20

Above:
On Monday 22 September 1958 'B12/3' No 61571 runs light-engine through Sheringham station; with round-topped firebox, it is in this condition that 'B12s' are best remembered. *Roger Harrison*

Beardmore engines were delivered in a slightly different shade of grey, lined-out in white.

Following the Grouping, the first Great Eastern locomotive to appear in apple green was No 1534, but it was several years before the sombre grey livery was eliminated from the 'B12s', for Stratford continued to use this colour-scheme for some time. However, the green livery survived the economies imposed by the LNER in 1928, but members of the class working in Scotland were painted black when they were shopped at Inverurie but with double red lining on the cab and tender sides — a livery not used on any other LNER class of locomotive. During World War 2 the 'B12s' were all turned out in unlined black livery, but following the cessation of hostilities the LNER adopted a policy of painting all of its locomotives in apple green. Between July 1946 and January 1947, Inverurie Works turned out six engines in green, and further members of the class were so treated as they passed through works.

A total of 72 'B12s' passed to British Railways upon Nationalisation; their new owner designated them mixed-traffic engines, which meant that they were painted in black lined in grey and straw, and both of the BR emblems were found upon the tenders. With the passage of time, however, the lining was often forgotten.

Right:
Holden GER Class S69 —
LNER Class B12, as built.

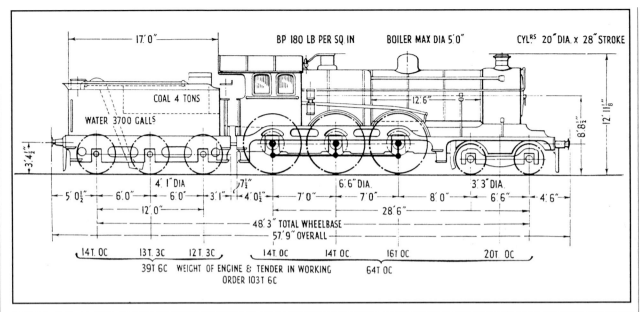

Right:
Holden GER Class S69 as
rebuilt to LNER Class
B12/3 with round-top
boiler.

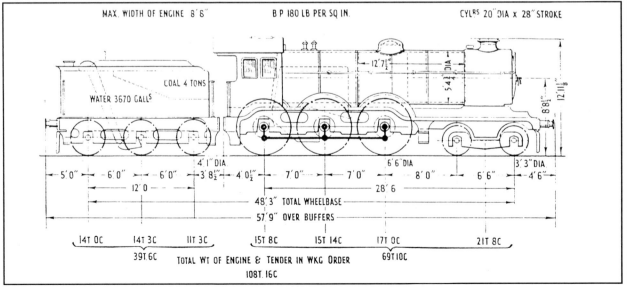

2. GREAT CENTRAL RAILWAY

The LNER classification of the ex-Great Central Railway 4-6-0s did not follow a logical pattern, and they are treated here in chronological order of construction.

Robinson Class 8 — LNER Class B5
6ft 1in engines

Class 8 was Robinson's first 4-6-0 design for the GCR, forming the basis for three later classes of the same wheel arrangement. Class 8 was originally intended for the fast movement of fish trains from Grimsby, this primary duty

earning the locomotives the title of 'Fish Engines', which lasted throughout their lives, but, notwithstanding their designer's original plans, they were seen on passenger trains in later years. Built with 6ft driving wheels, they are quoted as 6ft 1in engines due to thicker tyres fitted later in their careers.

The class saw the light of day in 1902 and ran to a total of 14 engines built in two batches, Nos 1067-72 coming from Neilson & Co under works numbers 6235-40 and a further eight, numbered 180-7, coming from Beyer, Peacock under works numbers 4531-8 in 1904. They were twin-cylinder (19x26in) saturated engines weighing 65 tons 2cwt; as built the class was equipped with the standard Robinson 3,250gal

Right:
Robinson GCR Class 8 —
LNER Class B5.

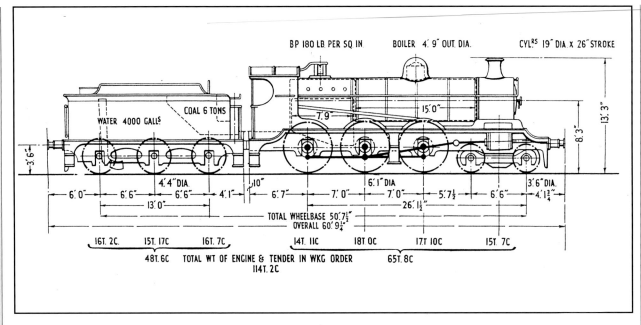

BP 180 LB PER SQ IN.   BOILER 4' 9" OUT. DIA.   CYL^{RS} 19" DIA X 26" STROKE

COAL 6 TONS

WATER 4000 GALL^S

15' 0"

7' 9"

13' 3"

8' 3"

3' 6"

4' 4" DIA.

6' 1" DIA.

3' 6" DIA.

6' 0" — 6' 6" — 6' 6" — 4' 1" — 10" — 6' 7" — 7' 0" — 7' 0" — 5' 7½" — 6' 6" — 4' 1¾"

13' 0"

26' 1½"

TOTAL WHEELBASE 50' 7½"

OVERALL 60' 9¼"

16T. 2C.   15T. 17C   16T. 7C   14T. 11C   18T. 0C   17T. 10C   15T. 7C

48T. 6C   TOTAL WT OF ENGINE & TENDER IN WKG ORDER   65T. 8C

114T. 2C

tender, which weighed 50 tons 2cwt. The 'fish engines' had never been intended to make long runs without water stops, but with the coming of water troughs on the Great Central they became an embarrassment with their small tenders, and the Running Superintendent decreed that 4,000gal tenders weighing 48 tons 6cwt should be substituted from other engines. This subsitution took place in 1905/6, and at the Grouping all 14 engines passed to the LNER (in whose ownership they became Class B5) with 4,000gal tenders. All were built with 4ft 9in-diameter boilers and no rebuilding took place under the Great Central, although superheating had been considered shortly before Grouping; six months into LNER ownership No 184 was fitted with a 5ft-diameter superheated boiler and became Class B5/2, the remainder being designated 'B5/1'. Subsequently all members of the class received superheated boilers of the original diameter, seven of them being fitted with 21in cylinders with piston valves and receiving the classification 'B5/3'. When the final two engines were superheated in 1935/6 the whole class was assimilated into this later classification, and in December 1937 the

subdivisions were abolished and the class reverted in its entirety to 'B5'. One locomotive was cut up in 1939, but with that exception all survived World War 2 and became British Railways property, but they were all withdrawn without being repainted or renumbered.

Numbering
The original GCR numbering of the class has been dealt with above. At the Grouping the Neilson-built engines were renumbered 6067-72 whilst those which came from Beyer, Peacock became 5180-7. Under the 1946 LNER renumbering scheme the 'B5s' were allocated numbers from 1300 to 1312, but only 1311 and 1312 were actually applied (in January 1946), for it soon became apparent that this series of numbers would be required for the new Thompson 'B1' class. As a result, a new series of numbers from 1678 to 1690 was allocated and applied by November 1946, the two engines which received their 13xx numbers being the first to receive their 1600 numbers, in March. BR numbers with 60,000 added to the final LNER numbers were allotted but, as mentioned

Left:
Class B5 (GCR Class 8) represented Robinson's first 4-6-0 design for the GCR. A total of 14 were built from 1902 to 1904, primarily for fast fish trains between Grimsby and London, resulting in the class's nickname of 'Fish Engines'. No 182 was one of eight built by Beyer, Peacock in 1904. It became No 5182 at the Grouping, was superheated in April 1933 and was renumbered 1307 (never carried) and 1685 in 1946, ultimately being withdrawn in March 1948 without ever carrying its allotted BR number (61685).
Ian Allan Library

above, were never applied, which is a little surprising given that the final member of the class (No 1686) was not withdrawn until June 1950.

Liveries

The GCR's passenger-locomotive livery consisted of the company's own distinctive shade of Brunswick green, with the wheel splashers and the sides of the running plate finished in Indian lake. Under LNER ownership these locomotives were initially painted as goods engines in black with red lining, but the lining was discontinued in 1928 when the company instituted economies. The practice had been reintroduced by 1939, and during the war the brass beading around the splashers was usually kept polished and was not painted over. The beading was removed from No 184 when rebuilding took place in June 1923 and from 6070 in June 1931.

Right:
The first six 'B5s' were built by Neilson & Co in 1902. GCR No 1070 was built in December 1902, became LNER No 6070 at the Grouping and was superheated in May 1936. Despite the relatively late date — No 6070 was the last of the class to be superheated — the locomotive was the first of the class to be withdrawn, succumbing in March 1939; the remainder survived until May 1947 at the earliest. *Ian Allan Library*

Below right:
During the period 1926-36 the entire 'B5' class was rebuilt with the superheated boiler as fitted to the Class Q4 0-8-0s. The modifications also included shorter chimneys, a flattened dome and relocated whistle. No 1689, rebuilt in January 1928, illustrates the changed lines to good effect at Mexborough shed on 17 April 1949. This locomotive had originally been built by Beyer, Peacock in February 1904 as GCR No 186, becoming LNER No 5186 at the Grouping and being renumbered 1311 (carried) and 1689 in 1946. Although allocated BR number 61689, this was not carried prior to withdrawal in October 1949. *D. Trevor Rowe*

Left:
Until the appearance of the first Class 8C (LNER Class B1 — later B18) in 1903, the Great Central had relied upon 4-4-0s for its express-passenger services. Two 4-6-0s, Nos 195 and 196, were built to a design of Robinson by Beyer, Peacock in December 1903 and January 1904. Fitted with 6ft 9in driving wheels, the locomotives were built for comparison with Atlantics over the main line to London. Robinson concluded that 4-6-0s were more successful than 4-4-2s, with the result that he produced a number of additional 4-6-0 classes — of varying degrees of success — during his period as CME of the GCR. No 196, pictured here, was initially fitted with 19in-diameter cylinders — No 195 initially had cylinders half an inch larger — and was to become LNER No 5196 at the Grouping.
Ian Allan Library

Robinson Class 8C — LNER Class B1 (later B18) 6ft 9in engines

A class of just two locomotives might be described as an experiment and, should they not be identical, perhaps even more so. This was in fact the case with Nos 195 and 196, for Robinson decided upon some comparative trials between two new Atlantics (Nos 192 and 194 — LNER Class C4) and two 4-6-0s: the design work for the four engines was carried out by Beyer, Peacock, based upon Robinson's Class 8 (LNER B5) referred to above. Beyer, Peacock built the two 4-6-0s under Works Nos 4541 (195) and 4542 (196) in December 1903 and January 1904 respectively. They had beaded splashers over each driving wheel and were handsome engines but lacked the grace of the later Robinson 4-6-0s, which had continuous splashers. Class B1 were twin-outside-cylinder locomotives. No 195 had cylinders measuring 21x26in with Stephenson motion employing 10in piston valves producing a tractive

effort of 21,658lb. By contrast No 196 had 19x26in cylinders, Stephenson motion with slide valves and a tractive effort of 17,729lb. The former weighed 72 tons 18cwt and the latter exactly 71 tons; as built they were equipped with 3,250gal tenders with water-scoops, but these were soon replaced with 4,000gal tenders from 0-8-0 engines. No 195 was superheated in 1912 but reverted to a saturated boiler in September 1920; it was again superheated in March 1926, and No 196 was superheated in April 1927.

Numbering
The original Great Central Railway numbering has been dealt with above. At the Grouping, both locomotives passed to the LNER, where they became Nos 5195 and 5196 in July 1924 and April 1925 respectively. These numbers were carried until the 1946 renumbering scheme when they were initially allocated Nos 1470 and 1471, but the imminent arrival of the Thompson 'B1s' dictated a need for these two numbers and the Robinson 'B1s' became Nos 1479 and 1480. The coming of the new Thompson engines (which their designer initially

Above:
No 196 is seen again in its post-Grouping guise as LNER No 5196. Both members of the class were modified during their careers by being superheated — No 196 in April 1927 — and both were also fitted with 21in cylinders (again, No 196 was treated in April 1927). They were reclassified as 'B18s' in 1943 to allow the new Thompson 4-6-0s to be classified 'B1'. Under the initial 1946 renumbering scheme, the pair were scheduled to become Nos 1470/1, but these numbers were never carried, and they were eventually renumbered 1479/80. Both locomotives were withdrawn in December 1947. *P. Ransome-Wallis*

instructed should be known 'as just Class B') resulted in the Robinson engines' being re-classified as 'B18'. Both survived two world wars but were withdrawn from Annesley in December 1947 and thus did not pass to British Railways.

Liveries
Under the LNER both engines were painted in apple green, which they retained under the 1928 economies; they eventually lost this scheme during World War 2, but the colour survived on No 5195 certainly until 1943 when they were painted black. The running-number was carried on the tender under the owner's initials and later on the cab sides, with 'LNER' in larger lettering retained upon the tender sides.

Left:
An extremely rare photograph of the only ex-Great Central Class B4 to receive postwar apple-green livery: in April 1947, at Ardsley shed, No 1482 *Immingham* is seen with unshaded sans-serif lettering. No 1482, built at Beyer, Peacock in June 1906, was one of only four members of the class to be allocated a BR number — the others being Nos 1483/5/8 — but, like the other three, did not last long enough for the new number to be applied. It was withdrawn in November 1950, being the last of the class to survive and outliving the penultimate member of the class by more than a year. *David Jenkinson/ Colour-Rail (NE93)*

Robinson Class 8F 'Immingham' — LNER Class B4
6ft 7in engines

Class 8F (not to be confused with Stanier's much later usage of the classification for the London, Midland & Scottish Railway) was a development of the experimental Class 8C (LNER B1/B18) and was identical to that class except that the '8F' had 3in smaller driving wheels. This difference was later reduced to 2in with the fitting of thicker tyres. The class consisted of 10 locomotives built by Beyer, Peacock under Order No 9458 and Works Nos 4816-25, all being delivered in June and July 1906 and employing running-numbers 6095-6104. As built they were saturated engines, with two outside 19x26in cylinders employing Stephenson motion with slide valves; they weighed 70 tons 14cwt and with their 4,000gal tenders tipped the scales at exactly 119 tons, producing a tractive effort of 18,178lb. They had splashers over each driving wheel. All 10 engines were superheated by the LNER, some receiving 21in-diameter cylinders with piston valves; this increased their weight to 71 tons 15cwt and their total with tender to 121 tons 1cwt, and raised their tractive effort to 22,106lb. This was marked by a sub-division of the class: the 21in cylinder engines became 'B4/1' and the 19in examples 'B4/2'. Despite the comparatively large driving wheels, the '8F' was originally intended for working fast goods and fish trains, and the class was initially used on this traffic between London, Manchester and Grimsby, but the engines were never strangers to passenger work. When the new dock at Immingham was opened in July 1906 No 1097 was selected to haul the special train conveying the management and guests to the ceremony; the locomotive was

named *Immingham* to mark the occasion and the class became
known by that name. It was the first GCR 4-6-0 to be named,
and remained the only member of this class to be so honoured.
All were equipped with standard GCR 4,000gal tenders. The
class was long-lived, all surviving until 1939, when No 6095
was withdrawn in July only to be reinstated in the October
owing to the outbreak of war and the expected increased call
upon the railways; it then survived until 1944, when it was
withdrawn following a collision.

Numbering
At the Grouping the locomotives were renumbered 6095-6104
and under the original 1943 scheme should have become

1490-9 but eventually became 1481-9; of these, Nos 1482,
1483, 1485 and 1488 passed to British Railways, but none was
renumbered. No 1482 *Immingham* survived until 1950 in
LNER apple-green livery.

Liveries
The '8Fs' were painted in GCR green when new but were soon
repainted black; under LNER ownership, however, green livery
was restored and lasted until the universal application of black
during World War 2. No 1482 *Immingham* alone among normal
ex-GCR 4-6-0s regained its green livery after the war but now
with Gill Sans lettering, although the Thompson rebuild of
No 6166 also received apple green.

Left:
Pictured in 1938 at the head of the 'North Country Continental' from Newcastle to Harwich at Escrick is 'B4' No 6104, which was the last of the class to be built (in July 1906). At the time, three of the class were shedded at Lincoln to haul the York–Lincoln section of this service. By the date of this photograph, all the members of the class had been superheated and six, including No 6104, had been fitted with 21in cylinders. *Ian Allan Library*

Right:
Pictured towards the end of its life, with final LNER number, No 1489 is seen at Pyewipe Junction, Lincoln, on 19 April 1947. This is again No 6104; under the original renumbering schedule of 1946 the locomotive should have become 1499, but in the event it was renumbered 1489, the class being renumbered 1481-9. No 1489 would not see Nationalisation, being withdrawn in July 1947. *H. C. Casserley*

Robinson Class 8G — LNER Class B9 5ft 4in engines

Beyer, Peacock & Co's Works Order No 9456 called for 10 4-6-0s which were built under Works Nos 4806-15, emerging with running numbers 105-14 in September and October 1906, immediately after completion of Class 8F. They were of generally similar design to their immediate predecessors but with 15in smaller driving wheels. The coupled wheels had individual splashers and there was a 'step' in the footplating over the 19x26in outside cylinders: the tractive effort was 22,438lb and they weighed 115 tons 12cwt with standard GCR 4,000gal tenders. They were built with saturated 5ft-diameter boilers, but sub-division of the class occurred when superheating took place under the LNER; those so treated became Class B9/2, the originals B9/1. All were converted by April 1929, but it was not until December 1937 that the 'B9/2' classification was dropped, the entire class reverting to 'B9'.

Numbering
Upon becoming LNER property, the '8G'/'B9' class had 6,000 added to their Great Central numbers, becoming Nos 6105-14. The 1943 renumbering scheme had a more marked effect upon them than on any other class of GCR 4-6-0: originally allocated 1342-51, they actually became 1469-78 when the system came into effect in 1946. Nos 1469, 1470, 1475 and 1476 survived to become British Railways property but only Nos 1469 and 1475 physically had 60,000 added to their numbers. This happened in February 1949 at Heaton Mersey shed, Stockport; the other two had been withdrawn during 1948.

Liveries
It would appear that these locomotives spent their entire lives in black livery in both GCR and LNER ownership. None of them ever acquired British Railways livery.

Above:
Constructed in September and October 1906 at Beyer, Peacock to a design by Robinson, the 'B9' (GCR '8G') class comprised 10 locomotives originally numbered 1105-14. No 1107, pictured here in 1911 at the head of a down express passing Abbey Lane Sidings at Leicester, was the third of the class to be built. The locomotive became LNER No 6107 after Grouping, and was renumbered 1344 (never carried) and 1471 in 1946; it was withdrawn from service in November 1947. *Ian Allan Library*

Right:
LNER No 6106 was the second of the class to be built, as GCR No 1106 in 1906. The locomotive was superheated in January 1926 and was renumbered 1343 (never carried) and 1470 under the LNER renumbering scheme of 1946. *Ian Allan Library*

Right:
Robinson GCR Class 8G — LNER Class B9.

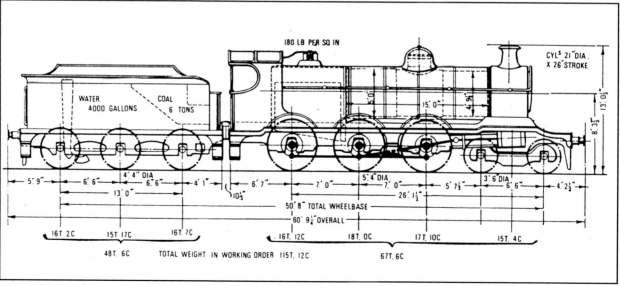

Robinson Class 1 — LNER Class B2 (later Class B19) 6ft 9in engines

Late in 1912 the first of Robinson's fifth class of 4-6-0 for the Great Central Railway emerged from Gorton Works. It was strikingly different from his previous four classes built to this wheel arrangement. Whereas its predecessors had all been outside-cylinder designs, Class 1 employed inside cylinders measuring 21½x26in (the largest ever fitted to an inside-cylinder engine in the UK), matched to a 5ft 6in-diameter superheated boiler (the first Robinson 4-6-0 to be built with one) with a heating surface inferior only to that of the country's sole Pacific then in existence, *The Great Bear* on the Great Western Railway. The first of the new class was numbered 423 and named *Sir Sam Fay* after the GCR's

General Manager. The new locomotive had the usual arc-roofed GCR-pattern cab and continuous splashers for the driving wheels over a raised running plate. It was an extremely handsome locomotive, enhanced with a copper-capped chimney as it was intended to exhibit it at the Ghent Exhibition. No 423 was quickly followed by four more of the class, the sixth member following only after an inexplicable delay. They were consecutively numbered; Nos 424 to 427 were unnamed when built but No 428 was named *City of Liverpool* from new. During June 1913 the remainder of the class were named: 424 *City of Lincoln*; 425 *City of Manchester*; 426 *City of Chester*; 427 *City of London*. The Great Central Railway having been born in Sheffield it is more than a little surprising that no locomotive was named after it nor yet after Nottingham; the explanation probably lies in the publicity-conscious railway company's wishing to emphasise the full extent of its network. No 427 lost its nameplates in

September 1937 when the name was taken for the 'B17/5' used to haul the 'East Anglian'.

The old adage that 'handsome is as handsome does' could sadly not be applied to the 'B2s', for the performance of these engines did not match their magnificent appearance. There were several weaknesses in the design, leading to poor performance which resulted in their being relegated to secondary expresses 'twixt Cleethorpes, Lincoln and Manchester, the London trains being entrusted to 'Director' 4-4-0s; appearances of 'B2s' on the London Extension were, to say the least, infrequent. As built, the 'B2' delivered a tractive effort of 22,700lb; some were built with and rebuilt with 20in-diameter cylinders giving a tractive effort of 19,644lb; all had Stephenson motion with 10in piston valves and weighed 123½ tons. All were equipped with the standard GCR 4,000gal tender. Despite their shortcomings they survived two world wars, lasting until 1947; their longevity may be attributed partly to the poverty of the LNER, which was loth to dispose of any engine from which some revenue-earning work could still be extracted, and World War 2 itself may have added a few years to their lives, as was the case with most of the ex-GCR 4-6-0s.

Numbering
Numbering by the GCR is detailed above: at the Grouping the six 'B2s' became Nos 5423-8, whilst under the 1943 LNER renumbering scheme they were allocated 1472-7, but, before the scheme was actually effected in 1946, two of the class had been withdrawn and the survivors eventually became Nos 1490-3. In 1945, when Edward Thompson began rebuilding some of Gresley's 'B17s' and classified them 'B2', the Robinson 'B2s' were reclassified as 'B19s'. No 1492 was the

Right:
The first of Robinson's 'B2' class to be constructed was No 423 in December 1912. The locomotive was named after the then General Manager of the GCR, Sir Sam Fay, and was fitted with a number of non-standard features, as it was initially intended that it would be displayed at an exhibition in Ghent. In the event a model of the locomotive was sent, and certain of the features, including a copper-capped chimney, were removed prior to World War 1. The locomotive became No 5423 at Grouping, being renumbered 1472 (never carried) and 1490 in 1946, before withdrawal in April the following year.
LNER

Right:
Robinson GCR Class 1 — LNER Class B2 (later Class B19).

last to be withdrawn, in November 1947, so none passed into British Railways ownership.

Liveries

No 423 emerged from Gorton Works adorned in the standard Great Central Railway passenger-locomotive livery of Brunswick green with Indian lake splashers and running boards and embellished (as mentioned above) with a copper-capped chimney, which was removed before Grouping. What followed was strange indeed: Nos 424, 426 and 427 were turned out in GCR goods-engine livery of black with red lining, whilst 425 and 428 were painted like 423. In LNER ownership the 'B2s' were painted in the standard passenger-locomotive livery of apple green lined in black and white, the running-number appearing on the tender sides below small 'LNER' lettering and, in later days, on the cabsides, with larger notation of ownership on the tender. Under wartime economy measures they were painted black with 'NE' on the tender sides.

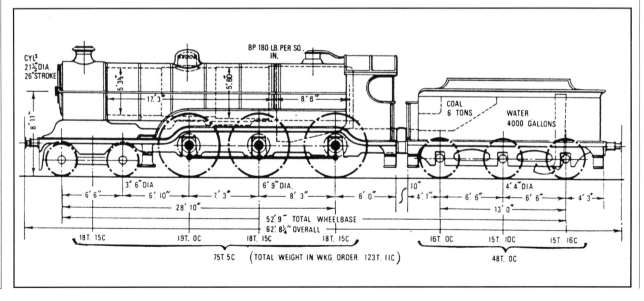

Robinson Class 1A — LNER Class B8
5ft 7in engines

The first member of this class was named *Glenalmond*, and it was by that name that they were known from their introduction in 1913, just one year after Class 1/B2 upon which they were based, though with smaller driving wheels. A further year elapsed before the second member of the class appeared, the first of a batch of 10 (the overall total being 11), the last of which was built in January 1915. The twin inside cylinders measured 21½x26in with Stephenson motion and 10in piston valves. In common with all GCR 4-6-0s, the boilers were pressed to 180lb/sq in, and their tractive effort was 27,445lb; they were also the first class to be fitted by Robinson with top feed. Tender equipment was the standard GCR 4,000gal variety. Sadly the shortcomings of the 'Sir Sam Fay' series were perpetuated, and the '1As'/'B8s' spent their lives mainly on goods trains, with some slow passenger work and the occasional excursion. The only significant rebuilding was the fitment of Unolco oil firing to Nos 279, 443 and 445 in June 1921.

Naming and Numbering
The GCR's numbering of this class can best be described as haphazard: the first example was numbered 4, the next eight (built between July and November 1914) received numbers 439-46; the final two emerged from Gorton in November 1914 and January 1915 and were numbered 279 and 280! In 1924 the GCR numbers were advanced by 5,000, and in 1943 the class was allocated 1331-41, but by the time 1946 and the great renumbering came about they received numbers 1349-59 under the revised scheme. Nos 1353-5/7/8 survived to see Nationalisation, but none received its BR number.

Four members of the class were named; as already mentioned, the first was named *Glenalmond* after the Scottish home of the Chairman of the GCR, Sir Alexander Henderson, whilst No 439 received the name of the home of one of the directors, *Sutton Nelthorpe*. No 279 was named *Earl Kitchener of Khartoum* — fully understandable, as he was Secretary of State for War at the time — but the choice of *Earl Roberts of Kandahar* (No 446) is less obvious, as his fame had been achieved in the Boer War. The nameplates of all four engines were carried on the top of the long, straight splashers.

Liveries
Being passenger locomotives, the class received GCR Brunswick green with Indian lake embellishments and, later, in LNER ownership, apple green.

Right:
Reflecting the wartime environment in which the majority of the class was built, two of the locomotives were named after British military leaders. No 279, the penultimate member of the class to be constructed (in December 1914), was named after Earl Kitchener. The locomotive became LNER No 5279 at Grouping, and then successively 1340 (never carried) and 1358 under the 1946 renumbering scheme. Allocated BR number 61358, the locomotive was withdrawn in August 1948 before receiving it.
Ian Allan Library

Above far right:
Pictured again in its final LNER state at Hull on 17 April 1947, No 1349 *Glenalmond* was nearing the end of its career. As was the case with many locomotives, World War 2 had both extended its life and expanded its area of operation as wartime exigencies broke down traditional operating areas. No 1349, for example, found itself in Edinburgh on at least one occasion during the war.
A. F. Cook

Right:
Robinson GCR Class 1A, — LNER Class B8.

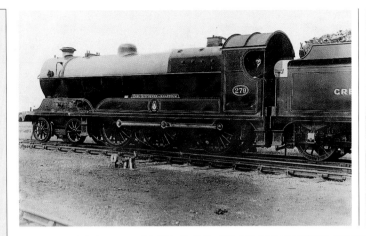

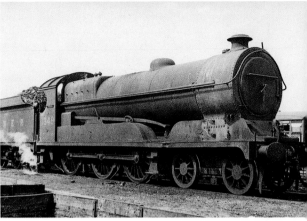

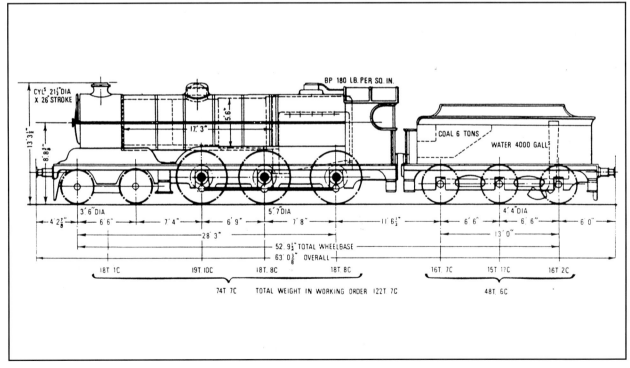

Robinson Class 9P — LNER Class B3
6ft 9in engines

Following the emergence of Class 1/B2, it would be four years before Robinson's largest passenger design for the GCR was to see the light of day, in 1917. Construction of the remaining five members of the class then took place in 1920. In contrast to the previous five classes of 4-6-0, the '9Ps' had four cylinders, each of which measured 16x26in; they employed Stephenson motion with 8in piston valves. The inside cylinders drove onto the front axle, with those outside powering the centre axle; tractive effort was 25,145lb. The locomotives weighed 127 tons 8cwt and were coupled to standard GCR 4,000gal tenders. Like the Class 1s/ B2s, the four-cylinder engines had straight splashers over the coupled wheels and were equally handsome save for the fact that the outside cylinders gave the front end a somewhat heavy appearance; from new they were equipped with superheated Belpaire boilers, which served to enhance their appearance. No rebuilding took place under the GCR but the LNER made

some alterations. Gresley rebuilt Nos 6166 and 6168 with Caprotti valve-gear in 1929 and Nos 6164 and 6167 in 1938/9, and they were classified 'B3/2' (the unmodified engines becoming 'B3/1'). Under Edward Thompson in 1943 No 6166 underwent a much more extensive rebuild, during which it lost all vestiges of its Robinson parentage. Only the bogie, driving wheels and the rear part of the frame behind the cylinders survived; to this rump was welded what was virtually a Thompson 'B1' front end, complete with cylinders and motion surmounted by a 'B1' boiler and cab. This rebuild was, for all practical purposes, a Thompson 'B1' with larger driving wheels (all else that survived was the GCR tender); it was classified 'B3/3' but was not a success.

Numbering

As built by the Great Central, this class of six locomotives was numbered 1169, 1164-8, and all were named. The first was named *Lord Faringdon* after the then Chairman of the company; this gentleman may be unique in having two locomotives named after him, the first 'Director' 4-4-0 being named *Sir Alexander Henderson* — his name before his

elevation to the House of Lords. Thereafter names were applied as follows: 1164 *Earl Beatty*; 1165 *Valour*; 1166 *Earl Haig* (removed upon rebuilding in October 1943); 1167 *Lloyd George*; 1168 *Lord Stuart of Wortley*. Of these, No 1165 deserves some special mention: *Valour* was the GCR War Memorial engine and carried large shield-shaped nameplates occupying almost the entire depth of the splashers and precluding the fitment of works plates, which were carried upon the cylinder covers. The legend on the nameplates read: 'In memory of G.C.R. employees who gave their lives for their country 1914-1918'. Until the outbreak of World War 2 it was traditional on every Armistice Day for the locomotive to work the 8.20am from London Road, Manchester, to Sheffield, conveying a party of railwaymen to a memorial service there, with the nameplates decorated with poppies. The balance of the names commemorated another director of the company (No 1168) and a soldier (1166), a sailor (1164) and statesman who had strong connections with the Great War (1167). The *Lloyd George* nameplates were abruptly removed in August 1923 at King's Cross upon the orders of Sir Frederick Banbury, the last Chairman of the Great Northern Railway, but what particular sin the Welshman had committed is not recorded. At the Grouping,

6,000 was added to the GCR numbers; then, under the 1943 renumbering scheme, the 'B3s' were allocated 1480-5 but when the scheme came into effect in 1946 were given numbers 1494-9. No 6168 was withdrawn in 1946 without actually being renumbered. All but one were withdrawn prior to Nationalisation, the exception being the Thompson rebuild, which became 61497 in April 1948 and was withdrawn exactly a year later.

Liveries

The GCR painted the Class 9Ps in its glorious passenger-locomotive livery. Post-Grouping, this was replaced by LNER apple green, which lasted until 1941 when all were outshopped in unlined black; this was retained after the war, with 'NE' on the tender, but Nos 1494 and 1496 had this changed to the full 'LNER'. When rebuilt in October 1943 No 6166 was painted unlined black, with its numbers and 'NE' in shaded transfers, but in January 1947 (by which time it had been renumbered 1497) it was repainted at Gorton Works in full LNER apple green with numbers and lettering in unshaded Gill Sans. In April 1948 the locomotive was again ex works and retained apple-green livery, albeit now numbered 61497 and with 'BRITISH RAILWAYS' tender lettering.

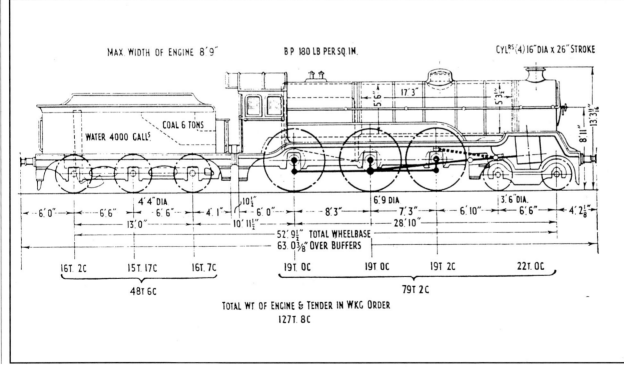

MAX. WIDTH OF ENGINE 8´9˝   B.P. 180 LB PER SQ. IN.   CYL^RS (4) 16˝DIA x 26˝STROKE

17´3˝

5´6˝

5´3¼˝

13´3¹¹⁄₁₆˝

8´11˝

COAL 6 TONS

WATER 4000 GALL^S

4´4˝DIA   6´9 DIA   3´6˝DIA.

10¹⁄₂˝

← 6´0˝ → ← 6´6˝ → ← 6´6˝ → ← 4´1˝ → ← 6´0˝ → ← 8´3˝ → ← 7´3˝ → ← 6´10˝ → ← 6´6˝ → ← 4´2¹⁄₈˝ →

13´0˝

10´11¹⁄₂˝

28´10˝

52´9¹⁄₂˝ TOTAL WHEELBASE
63´0³⁄₈˝ OVER BUFFERS

16T. 2C   15T. 17C   16T. 7C   19T. 0C   19T. 0C   19T. 2C   22T. 0C

48T 6C   79T 2C

TOTAL WT OF ENGINE & TENDER IN WKG ORDER
127T. 8C

Far left:
The last of the 'B3' class to be constructed was No 1168 *Lord Stuart of Wortley*, which emerged from Gorton Works in October 1920. Pictured here in its early post-Grouping guise as LNER No 6168, the locomotive was rebuilt as a 'B3/2' with Caprotti valve-gear in September 1929 (the first to be so treated). Under the LNER renumbering scheme of 1946, it was initially allocated the number 1485 and then 1499, but neither was actually carried, and the locomotive was withdrawn in September 1946, the first of its class to be retired. *Ian Allan Library*

Above left:
GCR No 1169 *Lord Faringdon* was the first of the 'B3s' to emerge and was named after the company's then Chairman. The locomotive became LNER No 6169 at the Grouping, before being renumbered 1480 (never carried) and 1494 in 1946. Pictured here at Spalding on 16 April 1947, it was one of only two of the class not to receive Caprotti valve-gear and would be withdrawn in December 1947. *H. C. Casserley*

Left:
Robinson GCR Class 9P — LNER Class B3.

Robinson Class 8N — LNER Class B6
5ft 8in engines

The first member of this class emerged from Gorton Works in July 1918 numbered 416, which lay in the middle of the series of Class 8M 2-8-0s (LNER Class O5) with identical boiler, motion and 21x26in outside cylinders. No 416 remained the sole member of Class 8N for nearly three years, until Nos 52 and 53 were constructed in March and April of 1921. The motion was Stephenson with 10in piston valves, the tractive effort was 25,798lb and the weight was 121 tons 4cwt with the standard GCR 4,000gal tender with water pick-up apparatus and coal capacity of 6 tons. The '8Ns'/ 'B6s' had straight footplating with the splashers extending the full length of the driving wheels. They were employed on both passenger and goods work, though intended as freight engines.

Numbering
On becoming LNER property at the Grouping, GCR Class 8N became LNER Class B6 and the locomotives had 5,000 added to their numbers, becoming Nos 5052, 5053 and 5416; under the 1943 renumbering scheme they were allocated 1328-30 respectively but instead became 1346-8 in 1946. None survived to become British Railways property, the class leader being withdrawn in November 1947 and the other two in December.

Liveries
The '8Ns'/'B6s' were painted black throughout their lives.

Right:
Robinson GCR Class 8N — LNER Class B6.

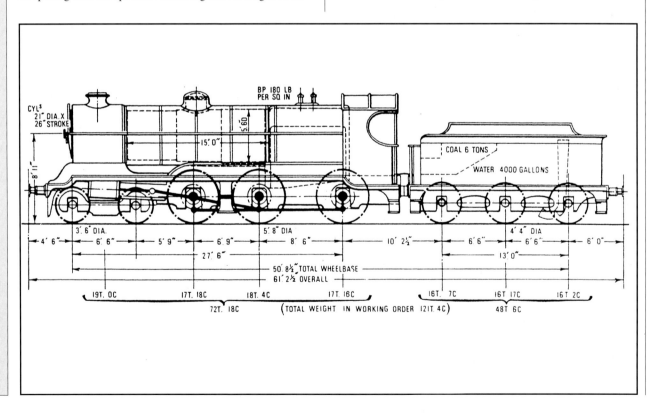

Above:
The smallest of the various 4-6-0 classes inherited by the LNER from the GCR was Class B6 (GCR Class 8N), consisting of three locomotives built from 1918 to 1921. The second of the trio, No 52 (pictured here), emerged from Gorton in March 1921. Initially allocated to Woodford Halse and used on services between Banbury and Sheffield, the locomotive was reallocated to Gorton when replaced by the later Class B7s. Whilst based at Gorton, the trio's regular duties included overnight freight services to Hull. After a sojourn at Sheffield, the locomotives were transferred away from GC metals to Ardsley and Bradford and then spent the rest of their careers based at either Sheffield or Ardsley. No 52 became LNER No 5052 at Grouping and then 1329 (never carried) and 1347 in 1946, before being withdrawn in December 1947. The 'B6' class was extinct prior to Nationalisation. *Ian Allan Library*

Right:
A total of 38 Robinson-designed 'B7' (GCR '9Q') class locomotives were constructed in the years 1921-4. Of these, 28 were built prior to the Grouping (Class B7/1) and 10 thereafter (Class B7/2). Designed as mixed-traffic locomotives, they had a reputation as heavy users of coal. Despite their small driving wheels — 5ft 8in — they were relatively fast and were regular performers on excursion trains. No 461 was one of 10 constructed at Vulcan Foundry in 1921, becoming LNER No 5461 after Grouping and being renumbered 1369 in 1946. Initially allocated BR number 61369, the locomotive was withdrawn in August 1948. *Ian Allan Library*

Far right:
Robinson GCR Class 9Q — LNER Class B7.

Robinson Class 9Q — LNER Class B7
5ft 8in engines

Robinson's final 4-6-0 for the GCR was a mixed-traffic design, examples of which emerged from Gorton in 1921 at monthly intervals in May, June and July, numbered 72, 73 and 78. Vulcan Foundry then built 10 under Works Order Nos 3478-87, the engines being numbered 36-8, 458-64, from September to November of the same year, whilst Gorton erected Nos 465 and 466 in August and October. There was then a brief lull until February 1922, when No 467 appeared, and the series continued through to No 474 in October. Meanwhile Beyer, Peacock & Co began construction of five in July 1922, starting with No 31 under Works Order 6107; 32 also came in July, under Works Order 6108, and 33-5 were built under Works Orders 6109-11 in August. Class 9Q/B7 was the only GCR 4-6-0 to see construction post-Grouping, Gorton constructing a final batch of 10, numbered 475-82 and 5483/4, between August 1923 and March 1924, bringing the class total to 38. This final batch had cab and boiler mountings reduced to conform with the LNER loading-gauge; the original engines were classified 'B7/1' and the 10 new specimens 'B7/2'. Stephenson motion was employed with 8in piston valves, the four cylinders measuring 16inx26; the tractive effort was 29,952lb and they weighed 127 tons 16cwt. The standard 4,000gal tender was fitted up to No 5466, but Nos 5467-84 had the final version with self-trimming bunker. They had straight splashers over the driving wheels and a 'step' in the footplating over the cylinders. The class gained a reputation as being heavy coal-consumers and such charming nicknames as 'Black Pigs' and 'Colliers' Friends'.

Numbering
None of the 'B7s' ever carried a name. Upon passing into LNER ownership, most 'B7s' had 5,000 added to their GCR numbers, the exceptions being Nos 5483 and 5484, which emerged new from works already carrying their LNER numbers. Uniquely amongst GCR 4-6-0s, the 'B7s' actually received the numbers allocated in 1943, the opportunity being taken to number them in a consecutive series from 1360 to 1397. They were also unique in being the only class of GCR 4-6-0 to pass in its entirety to British Railways at Nationalisation, when 60,000 was added to the 1946 LNER numbers. However, some further renumbering took place due to the continued production of Thompson 'B1s', 12 survivors being allocated numbers 61702-13 in April and May 1949, although No 61708 was withdrawn before its new number could be applied.

Liveries
Being mixed-traffic locomotives, members of this class were always painted black.

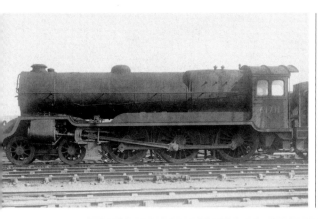

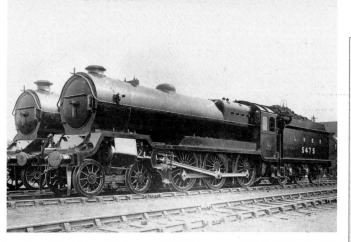

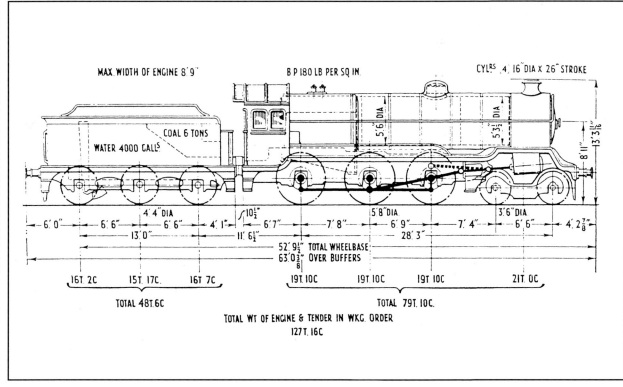

MAX. WIDTH OF ENGINE 8´9˝   B P 180 LB PER SQ IN.   CYLRS 4, 16˝ DIA X 26˝ STROKE

COAL 6 TONS

WATER 4000 GALLS

5´6˝ DIA

5´3½˝ DIA

13´3 3/16˝

8´11˝

6´ 0˝   6´ 6˝   4´ 4˝ DIA   6´ 6˝   4´ 1˝   10½˝   6´ 7˝   7´ 8˝   5´8˝ DIA   6´ 9˝   7´ 4˝   6´ 6˝   3´6˝ DIA   4´ 2 7/8˝

13´ 0˝   11´ 6½˝

52´ 9½˝ TOTAL WHEELBASE

63´ 0 3/8˝ OVER BUFFERS

28´ 3˝

16T. 2C   15T. 17C   16T. 7C   19T. 10C   19T. 10C   19T. 10C   21T. 0C

TOTAL 48T. 6C   TOTAL 79T. 10C.

TOTAL WT OF ENGINE & TENDER IN WKG. ORDER
127T. 16C

Far left:
Although all of the Class B7s remained in service at Nationalisation, withdrawals started shortly thereafter, and all had gone by July 1950. Of the 38 built, only 11 carried their final BR numbers, No 61711 becoming the final 'B7' in service. Seen here at Gorton on 10 April 1950, the locomotive had been built there in October 1923 as No 478, being renumbered 5478 in 1925 and then 1391 in 1946. It was the only member of the class to carry its original BR number (61391), before being again renumbered, this time in the 617xx sequence. *W. H. Whitworth*

Above left:
No 5475 was one of the 10 members of the class to be built, at Gorton, after the Grouping, emerging in August 1923. Renumbered 1388 in 1946, the locomotive was initially allocated BR number 61389 but was actually renumbered 61710 after the decision was taken to reserve the 613xx series for the new Thompson 'B1s' then under construction. The locomotive was to remain in service until February 1950, being one of the last ex-GCR 4-6-0s of its type to do so. *Ian Allan Library*

Above:
Colour pictures of ex-Great Central Class B7s enjoy a rarity approaching that of hens' teeth, but in August 1937 No 5474 was photographed in spotless LNER black livery at Neasden shed, with a well-filled tender, although the engine does not appear to be in steam. This view gives a good impression of the overall appearance of the 'B7' in LNER days; note the Works plate above the centre driving wheel on the straight splasher and the treatment of the footplating over the cylinder. The locomotive was built at Gorton in August 1922 and became LNER No 5474 at the Grouping; renumbered 1382 in 1946, it was to survive long enough to receive its BR number of 61707 two months before withdrawal in June 1949. *L. Hanson/Colour-Rail (NE43)*

Left:
Designated Class S by the NER and B13 by the LNER, a total of 40 locomotives of this Wilson Worsdell-designed type were built between 1899 and 1909 at Gateshead Works. No 2002, illustrated here, was the second to be built, in June 1899. This illustration shows the locomotive in its initial phase with single cab window; No 2002 was rebuilt in September 1901. Some of the first 10 locomotives were fitted with flangeless centre driving wheels; again, this proved unsatisfactory, and all ultimately received fully flanged wheels. No 2002 was superheated by the LNER in 1924 and would be withdrawn in July 1931. *Ian Allan Library*

3. NORTH EASTERN RAILWAY

These four classes of Worsdell and Raven North Eastern Railway 4-6-0s were classified by the LNER in the order in which they were introduced by the NER, from B13 to B16.

Wilson Worsdell Class S — LNER Class B13 6ft 1¼in engines

This class was the first British 4-6-0 passenger locomotive and the oldest class of that wheel arrangement inherited by the LNER. Construction of the first batch of 10 had commenced in 1899, the total of 40 locomotives being built 'in house' at Gateshead over the next 10 years to 1909: 10 in 1906, 10 in 1908 and the final batch spanning 1908 and 1909. The first three members of the class were numbered 2001-3 and were saturated engines with boilers pressed to 200lb/sq in

employing two outside cylinders, measuring 20x26in, and Stephenson motion with slide valves. With tenders of 3,700gal capacity they weighed exactly 101 tons and produced a tractive effort of 24,136lb. The total wheelbase was kept down to 48ft 4⅜in so that they could be turned on the existing 50ft turntables. These first three engines had shortened cabs in order to keep the whole engine within the constraints imposed by the turntables, but it was soon found that the disadvantages of the cramped cab outweighed the need to turn the engines on triangles, and they were all rebuilt in normal style at their first shopping. Superheating of the class commenced in 1913; thereafter the engines had piston valves, boiler pressure reduced to 160lb/sq in, 3,940gal tenders and tractive effort of 19,309lb, and weighed 106 tons 4cwt. Withdrawal began in August 1928, and all had gone from traffic by October 1938.

Numbering

As they emerged from Gateshead in 1899 and 1900 the first batch was numbered consecutively from 2001 to 2010. The second batch built in 1906 bore a random selection of numbers — 726/40/57/60/1/3/6/8/75, 1077; the 10 built from June to October 1908 were allocated 738/9/41/3-9. The final 10, built from November 1908 to March 1909, were almost consecutively numbered — 750-6/8/9/62. These numbers were retained at the Grouping. Only one 'B13' survived to see the 1943 renumbering, No 761 becoming 1699 in October 1946 and surviving as service stock until May 1951, having been officially withdrawn in September 1934. It was allocated BR number 61699S in departmental stock.

Liveries

When new, all 40 locomotives were painted in NER fully-lined green livery, but by the outbreak of World War 1 all were painted black. Nos 2009 and 2010 had been enhanced with gold lining to work the Royal Train from York to Newcastle in 1900, and in the same year No 2006 went to the Paris Exhibition, where it won the Grand Prize and gold medal. In LNER ownership the 'Ss' were reclassified 'B13' and painted black with red lining until 1928, when economies dictated plain black. However, No 2006 was singled out for further glory in 1925, when it was painted in full LNER passenger livery of white-and-black-lined apple green to take part in the Darlington Centenary cavalcade.

Right:
Pictured at Alnmouth, No 754 was one of the last batch of Worsdell's Class B13 to be built, emerging from Gateshead Works in January 1909. The locomotive is in the standard NER green livery in which locomotives of the class were painted prior to World War 1. By 1914, the class's livery had been altered to black. The picture shows clearly the two-window cab and the plated coal-rails on the tender. No 754 was superheated by the LNER in 1922 and withdrawn in December 1936.
Ian Allan Library

Pictured in the black livery that became standard for the type immediately prior to World War 1, No 775 was the penultimate example of the second batch to be built, emerging from Gateshead Works in August 1906. It was fitted with a superheater in December 1920 and was withdrawn in August 1936.
Ian Allan Library

Left:
Wordsell NER Class S — LNER Class B13.

CYL^RS 20"DIA. X 26"STROKE   BOILER 4'9"DIA.   B.P 200 LB PER SQ IN.

13'0"

8'2"

15'0"   8'0"   COAL 5 TONS   WATER 3700 GALL^S

3'6"

3'7"DIA.   6'1"DIA.   3'9"DIA.

1'9" 2'6" 6'6" 5'6½" 7'0" 7'0" 4'10" 5'5⅜" 6'0" 6'0" 4'0" 1'9"

26'0½"   12'0"

TOTAL WHEELBASE 48'4⅜"

58'4⅜" OVERALL

16T. 3C   11T. 19C   19T. 7C   14T. 19C

62T. 8C   TOTAL WT OF ENGINE & TENDER IN WKG ORDER   38T. 12C

101T. 0C.

Above:
Colour photography came too late to record the locomotives of the pre-Grouping companies in all their glory, but some enlightened photographers did have the foresight to record them when they had passed into the ownership of the 'Big Four'. One such example was ex-NER Class B13 No 761, seen at York shed in 1937. We are doubly fortunate in that this was the counter-pressure testing locomotive and is coupled to the dynamometer car with testing equipment fitted to the left cylinder. The locomotive is finished in LNER mixed-traffic livery of lined black with the number and class on the buffer-beam; no doubt the home shed is also there but is masked by the left-hand buffer. *H. M. Lane/Colour-Rail (NE163)*

Wilson Worsdell Class S1 — LNER Class B14
6ft 8¼in engines

Worsdell's second 4-6-0 class ran to a total of five engines and were built at Gateshead between December 1900 and August 1901. They had two outside cylinders measuring 20x26in with Stephenson motion and 8¾in piston valves; their saturated boilers were pressed to 200lb/sq in. Equipped with 3,940gal tenders, they weighed 108 tons 4cwt and produced a tractive effort of 22,069lb. All were superheated with Schmidt superheaters when new boilers were required between October 1913 and April 1917, with boiler pressure reduced to 175lb; in this condition the tractive effort was 19,310lb. All passed into LNER ownership, but withdrawal began in June 1929; the last went in April 1931, just two months short of 30 years old.

Numbering
The class took numbers 2111-5, these being retained after the Grouping.

Liveries
The class was originally painted in full NER lined green; from 1912 this was replaced by black lined in white, gold and red, but wartime economies dictated that by the time of the Grouping they were in goods-engine black with single red lining. Under their new owner they were accorded the distinction of apple green with the number on the tender, and it was in this condition that they were all withdrawn.

Raven Class S2 — LNER Class B15
6ft 1¼in engines

In 1910 Vincent Raven took over from Wilson Worsdell as Chief Mechanical Engineer of the North Eastern Railway, and with him came a transition in the company's locomotive affairs. Whereas the 'S' and 'S1' classes had been designed as passenger locomotives, the 'S2' was intended as a mixed-traffic engine. Hitherto the NER had relied heavily upon two cylinders, but Raven chose three for his larger engines — which may go some way to explaining why the 'S2' class ran to only 20 examples. They closely resembled their 'S1' predecessors but with deeper frames at the front, the first emerging from Darlington (where they were all erected) in 1911, with construction lasting over the next two years. The first seven were saturated, their boilers pressed to 180lb/sq in; their twin outside cylinders measured 20x26in with Stephenson piston-valve motion, producing a tractive effort of 21,723lb, and they weighed in at 109 tons 9cwt. From the eighth member of the class, the locomotives were superheated with Robinson superheaters, whereafter boiler pressure was reduced to 160lb; weight was increased to 111 tons 16cwt, but tractive effort fell to 19,309lb. By 1917 boiler pressure of the superheated engines had been increased to 175lb and tractive effort to 21,155lb. The last member of the class, No 825, was particularly noteworthy, as it was built with Stumpf 'Uniflow' cylinders and until 1919 was the only locomotive running in Great Britain in this form, although the system was quite common on the Continent at the time. With the Grouping, all of the 'S2s' passed into LNER ownership, where they became Class B15, but none survived to see Nationalisation. Withdrawal was spread over 10 years, the first going in September 1937 and the last in December 1947.

Numbering
The 20 engines followed no logical numbering sequence: as they emerged from Darlington they were numbered 782/6-8/91/5-9, 813/5/7/9-25, and these numbers were retained at the Grouping. Under the Thompson renumbering scheme of 1943 the 15 survivors were allocated numbers 1313-27 but by the time the scheme was put into effect in 1946 a further seven had been withdrawn, and the numbers were required for the Thompson 'B1s'; the surviving 'B15s' were then allotted 1691-8, but only four were actually renumbered. In May 1946 No 819 became 1695, 820 became 1696 and 821 assumed 1697. Finally, in November 1946, No 815 became 1693.

Liveries
As built, the first six received NER green livery, but No 796 appeared in black, and the earlier examples were so painted when shopped. The LNER painted them black initially, with the number on the tender beneath 'LNER', but the numbers later moved to the cab sides, with ownership in larger lettering on the tenders. With the restrictions imposed by World War 2, ownership was shortened to 'NE' on plain, unlined black.

Above:
Built at Darlington in May 1912, Class B15 (NER Class S2) No 797 was the first of the 20 members of the class to be fitted from new with a superheater. Designed by Vincent Raven, the type was planned for mixed-traffic duties. The locomotives were fitted with larger-diameter boilers than the earlier 'S' class (5ft 6in rather than 4ft 9in) and also possessed a larger heating surface. No 797 was the member of the class normally used in comparative tests with the 'Uniflow' example (see the next illustration) and was to be withdrawn by the LNER in October 1937.
Ian Allan Library

Above:
Ex-NER Class B15 No 813 at York shed in 1937. This is the only known colour shot of a 'B15' in LNER livery. *H. M. Lane/Colour-Rail (NE164)*

Left:
When built, in March 1913, No 825 was fitted with Stumpf-type 'Uniflow' cylinders as shown here. The considerable changes to the design of the basic locomotive to accommodate the modified cylinders and Walschaerts valve gear are readily apparent. The primary aim was to eliminate condensation in the cylinders, and, in comparative tests with No 797, the modification proved useful. However, World War 1 was not an ideal time to experiment with further developments of the equipment, and it was not until 1919 that a further example — based on an Atlantic — appeared. However, the advantages of the modification did not exceed the disadvantages of increased maintenance, and in March 1924 No 825 was converted to conventional format. It was to remain in service until February 1944. *Ian Allan Library*

Right:
No 787 was the third of the 20 Class B15s to appear, being built at Darlington in February 1912. Superheated in June 1920, this view records the locomotive in the post-Grouping era. No 787 was renumbered 1314 under the first phase of the LNER 1946 renumbering, subsequently becoming No 1692, prior to withdrawal in December 1946. Latterly the surviving 'B15s' were to be based at Hull Dairycoates. In LNER ownership the type was to be seen operating over ex-GCR metals as well as the more traditional ex-NER lines.
Ian Allan Library

Raven Class S3 — LNER Class B16
5ft 8in engines

Raven's second 4-6-0 class for the NER eventually ran to 70 examples. All were erected at Darlington, 38 built by the parent company and a further 32 after Grouping by the LNER, although the orders had been placed by the NER. Raven's 'S3' was the culmination of 20 years of development of the 4-6-0 on the NER which had started in 1899 with Worsdell's 'S' class. By December 1919, when the first 'S3' appeared (designated as a 'fast goods engine', though in reality a mixed-traffic locomotive), the distillation which had occurred through Raven's taking the basics of the 'S' and adding a larger-diameter boiler and his gradual movement to three cylinders on his larger engines produced the longest-lived of the four classes of NER 4-6-0, all but one of them lasting to see

Nationalisation. Notwithstanding the plans to electrify the line between York and Newcastle, the North Eastern still had a need for powerful steam locomotives to handle the colossal amount of goods and mineral traffic from which the company derived the bulk of its income, as well as the not inconsiderable number of secondary passenger routes. November 1918 had seen the ordering of an initial batch of 10 'S3s', and a further 25 were ordered in March 1919, the first of them appearing in December of that year (as mentioned above); all were in service by June 1921. Two further batches of 10 were ordered in January and March 1922, only three of which had been delivered by the end of the year, the balance appearing post-Grouping. The order for the final 15 was placed on 14 November 1922, the last of which entered traffic in January 1924.

The 'S3' was built superheated with three 18½ x 26in cylinders driving onto the front coupled axle, Stephenson motion with 8¾in piston valves and boilers pressed to 180lb/sq in; tractive effort was quoted as 30,312lb, but this was corrected to 30,031lb in December 1924. They were equipped with 4,125gal tenders and weighed 124 tons 6cwt. All 70 locomotives passed into LNER ownership, becoming Class B16, and worked unaltered until 1937, when Gresley undertook substantial rebuilding of No 2364, incorporating his system of Walschaerts valve-gear with 9in piston valves for the outside cylinders and derived motion operating the inside one. This necessitated the movement of the bogie forward by 9in and lengthening the frames, and the opportunity was taken to fit a new cab and raise the running-plate over the wheels, all of which had a considerable impact upon the appearance of the locomotive. As rebuilt, it weighed 125 tons 6cwt and was designated 'B16/2', the originals being known thereafter as 'B16/1s'. Six more engines were similarly treated. From 1944 Thompson undertook further rebuilding, but these rebuilds had three sets of Walschaerts valve-gear, with 9in piston valves; 17 of the class were so treated up to 1949, weighing 125 tons 11cwt and designated 'B16/3'.

Numbering
As built, the first 10 of the class were numbered 840-9: the second batch of 25, built in 1920/1, were numbered 906/8/9/11/4/5/20-34/6/7/42/3. The third batch, built in 1922/3, carried numbers 2363-72; the 1923 batch of 10 were Nos 2373-82, whilst the final 15, of 1923/4, were numbered 1371-85. Under the 1943 renumbering scheme the 69 remaining engines (No 925 was a war casualty) were allocated numbers 1400-68, and these were applied to the locomotives between February 1946 and January 1947. Post-Nationalisation renumbering was somewhat more complicated: with the exception of Nos 1403, 1408 and 1409, all had their numbers enhanced by 60,000, but by December 1949 construction of the Thompson 'B1' class meant that the number sequence needed for these was encroaching upon the 'B16' numbers, and in that month the first 10 'B16s' (Nos 61400-9) were moved to the end of the class sequence, taking up numbers 61469-78 vacated by the scrapping of the 'B9' class. In practice, Nos 1403, 1408 and 1409 went directly to 61472, 61477 and 61478 instead of having 60,000 added to their respective LNER numbers. An interesting point was raised by this change: in some instances where smokebox numberplates had been fitted to the other seven engines, these were not immediately

changed, resulting in the locomotives' carrying differing smokebox and cabside numbers.

Liveries
All 70 engines were painted black with single red lining by both the NER and the LNER, but from 1928 the lining was abandoned as they passed through shops. In early LNER days the running-number was carried upon the tender, with the ownership in small lettering above it, but this was later superseded by cabside numbering, with 'LNER' in larger letters upon the tender. From 1950, British Railways accorded the 'B16s' red, cream and grey lining on black, and all 69 survivors received this livery

Above:
A 'B16' hard at work. Tuesday 8 September 1959 saw 'B16/1' No 61445 passing Spalding with a southbound freight; the mandatory wagon between the tender and the first tank-wagon is in evidence, but a bolster wagon put to such use is unusual. Roger Harrison

Above:
Class B16/3 (Thompson rebuild of Class B16) No 61444 is recorded at Doncaster (not far from its home shed of York) in October 1961 with the later BR emblem on the tender. Ignore the step in the footplating and the ex-NER tender and this could almost be a 'B1'. Behind the 'B16' stand two of Robert Riddles' designs — an ex-WD Austerity 2-8-0 and a BR '9F' 2-10-0 — whilst on the adjacent road stands Class K3/3 2-6-0 No 61887. *B. Metcalfe/Colour-Rail (BRE202)*

Left:
A year later, in 1962, the same locomotive looks somewhat more work-stained as it approaches Catesby Tunnel with a down fitted freight. No 61444 was one of the last of the class to survive, being withdrawn in June 1964.
J. P. Mullett/Colour-Rail (BRE1124)

Right:
Unusually clean, Raven-designed Class B16/1 No 61411 stands at its home shed Neville Hill, Leeds, in April 1960 wearing the later BR totem.
P. J. Hughes/Colour-Rail (BRE1195)

Above:
Class B16/1 No 61440 working hard as it passes through Staveley Central in 1955 with an up goods. The locomotive shows a remarkable lack of care, for there is scant evidence of a cabside number and practically none of a tender emblem; such was the lot of a freight locomotive. The signal which the train has just passed is already set back to danger.
David Swale

Right:
Class B16/1 No 61423 south of Bulwell Common in the early 1950s, heading for Nottingham Victoria with an empty-stock train. *David Swale*

Above:
Class B16/3 No 61449 passing Spalding with a southbound freight on Saturday 19 April 1952. Rebuilt by Edward Thompson with a 'B1' cab and Type 100A boiler, the locomotive bears little resemblance to its origins and, apart from the step in the footplating behind the cylinder, could at first glance be taken for a 'B1'. *Roger Harrison*

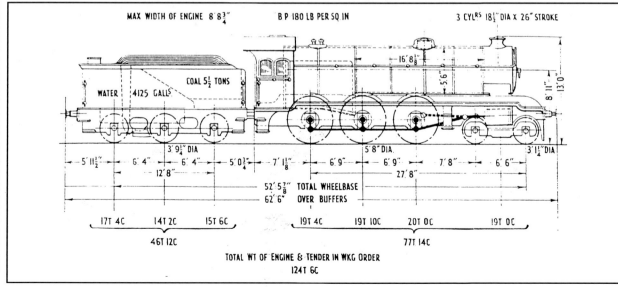

MAX WIDTH OF ENGINE 8'8¾"   B P 180 LB PER SQ IN   3 CYL^{RS} 18½" DIA X 26" STROKE

COAL 5½ TONS

WATER 4125 GALLS

16'8½"

5'6"

8'11"   13'0"

3'9¼" DIA   5'8" DIA   3'1¼" DIA

5'11½"   6'4"   6'4"   5'0¾"   7'1⅛"   6'9"   6'9"   7'8"   6'6"

12'8"   27'8"

52'5⅞" TOTAL WHEELBASE
62'6" OVER BUFFERS

17T 4C   14T 2C   15T 6C   19T 4C   19T 10C   20T 0C   19T 0C

46T 12C   77T 14C

TOTAL WT OF ENGINE & TENDER IN WKG ORDER
124T 6C

Left:
Raven NER Class S3 — LNER Class B16.

Above:
Class B16/2 (Gresley rebuild of Raven 'B16/1') No 61421 is pictured at Ferrybridge power station in 1962. The driver takes it easy as he watches the photographer at work. An excellent portrait shot of the class. *Colour-Rail (BRE1340)*

Above:
Unrebuilt Class B16/1 No 61456 stands at Haymarket shed, Edinburgh, in 1958. Compare the cab with that of the Gresley rebuild pictured opposite.
Colour-Rail (SC874)

Right:
With the gracious permission of HM King George V, No 2800, numerically the first 'B17/1', was named *Sandringham* after the Royal estate in Norfolk, but this locomotive was actually the third member of the class delivered into traffic at Stratford by the North British Locomotive Co Ltd, in December 1928 under Works No 23803. Pullman trains on the Great Eastern section of the LNER were rare, to say the least, but one such regular working was the 'Eastern Belle'. The up train left Clacton-on-Sea at 8.5pm and is seen on 11 June 1929 with *Sandringham* in charge. *Ken Nunn collection/ LCGB*

Just two completely new 4-6-0 classes were introduced by the London & North Eastern Railway — one each from its first two Chief Mechanical Engineers, the second of whom also rebuilt some of his predecessor's design into a new class.

Gresley Class B17 'Sandringham' 6ft 8in engines

Due to increasing loads, by 1926 the passenger-locomotive situation on the Great Eastern section of the LNER had reached critical proportions, as the Holden GER 'S69'/'B12' class was beginning to struggle, and something more powerful but similar in proportion to the available motive power was needed. However, this was a problem which would not be easily solved. The conditions imposed by the Civil Engineering Department — not least the permitted hammer-blow — and the continuing proliferation of short turntables dictated the overall length of the locomotive and tender and the permitted hammer-blow. The resultant specification which Gresley sent to Doncaster called for a locomotive 'to work over all Great Eastern lines', giving a tractive effort of c25,000lb, 30ft of grate area and a maximum axle load of 17 tons, with all three cylinders driving onto the

centre-coupled axle. In order to achieve the required aims Doncaster even went so far as to produce a drawing for a taper-boiler locomotive, but sadly this no longer exists. Doncaster eventually proved unequal to the task and the North British Locomotive Co undertook to produce the requisite design, but it too could not achieve all that was needed, and the amended requirement for the new engine became one calling for a locomotive capable of running 'over certain Great Eastern lines'. The first batch of 10 locomotives was ordered from North British under Order No L850 in February 1928, and what was numerically the third member of the class was the first delivered from Cowlairs Works for final inspection on 30 November of the same year. The whole class had three 17½x26in cylinders, those outside driving onto the centre-coupled axle and the centre cylinder driving onto the leading axle, resulting in that cylinder's being placed well forward. They were equipped with Walschaerts/Gresley motion with 8in piston valves, 3,700gal GER-pattern tenders and boilers pressed to 200lb/sq in, producing a tractive effort of 25,380lb. They had Westinghouse brakes to locomotive, tender and train, and the Westinghouse pump was mounted on the rear right-hand side of the smokebox. This first batch was designated 'B17/1'. The 'B17/2' was similar to the 'B17/1' but built by the LNER at Darlington and equipped with similarly pressured boilers bought-in from Armstrong Whitworth. These locomotives were also attached to GER-pattern tenders. The first 15 of this sub-class had Westinghouse brakes, but the remaining 18 had steam brakes to the locomotive and tender and vacuum to the train. Twelve were built in 1930, 15 in 1931 and six in 1933. Both 'B17/1' and 'B17/2' weighed 116 tons 1cwt. Class B17/3 ran to just five engines, built in 1935 to an order placed in November 1933, and were identical to their predecessors except that they had vacuum brakes to locomotive, tender and train; they weighed 116 tons 13cwt. The final new sub-class was 'B17/4', built primarily for use in the western section of the LNER's Southern Area; 14 were built at Darlington between March and June 1936 and the final 11 by Robert Stephenson & Co under Order No E161 between January and July 1937. The 'B17/4s' were dramatically different in appearance, as they were equipped with 4,200gal Group Standard tenders; otherwise they were similar to the earlier engines, and weighed 129 tons 5cwt.

The late 1930s saw a vogue for streamlined trains on the LNER and LMS and a half-hearted attempt on the GWR. (The SR remained aloof but would have its fling during World War 2.) In September 1937 two 'B17s' were selected to be streamlined in the style of the 'A4' Pacifics for hauling the 'East Anglian' between Liverpool Street and Norwich. The streamlined casing was fitted over the original boiler cladding, and in this condition the two engines weighed 133 tons 3cwt; they were classified 'B17/5'. There remained one further variant of the class: from August 1943 onwards, 57 'B17s' were fitted with improved 100A boilers, in which form they were designated 'B17/6'. Amongst these were the two 'B17/5s', which were de-streamlined in 1951. Boiler pressure on the initial 'B17/6' conversions was reduced to 180lb, with a consequent reduction in tractive effort to 22,842lb, but this was later increased to 225lb, giving a tractive effort of 24,865lb. However, the most drastic change came when, from 1945, Edward Thompson rebuilt 10 'B17s' as 'B2s', and these are dealt with separately.

Numbering and Naming

When introduced, the 'B17s' were numbered from 2800 through to 2872 and became known as '2800s'. Under the 1943 renumbering scheme they were allocated numbers 1600-72, which were applied between January 1946 and January 1947. The class passed in its entirety to British Railways ownership and 60,000 was added to the 1946

Above right:
No 2813 *Woodbastwick Hall* was the second of five 'B17/2s' delivered into traffic in October 1930; the property after which it was named was the home of Mr John Cator and is situated between Cromer and Norwich. This view of the locomotive on an express near Ipswich in 1937 shows to advantage the positioning of the centre cylinder, as well as the spacing of the front number and the class on the buffer-beam and the placing of the Works plate on the centre splasher, beneath the nameplate.
Photomatic (Wholesale) Ltd

Right:
No 2816 *Fallodon*, photographed at Stratford on 1 July 1939; this engine-only picture illustrates well the wheel spacings and the lining employed on the 'B17' class by the LNER.
Ken Nunn collection/LCGB

numbers, but enginemen still referred to the 'B17s' as '2800s'. The entire class was named; with the gracious permission of HM King George V, No 2800 was named *Sandringham*, and, in addition to being called '2800s', the 'B17s' were also nicknamed 'Sandies' as a result. The next 47 were named after stately homes which lay within LNER territory, but there was some renaming in later days. Nos 2848-72 were named after

Below:
War has taken its toll of the lovely roof-boarded teak stock as Class B17/4 No 2867 *Bradford* rolls an up express into Aylesbury in August 1940. It is difficult to tell whether the ravages wrought upon the railways have resulted in the engine's being painted in the economy wartime black; the indications are that it is still in apple green (albeit extremely dirty), for the club's colours have not been painted out as was the practice when unlined black livery was applied. Generally speaking, it was only from November 1941 that unlined black became the norm for locomotives of this class; from early 1942 the 'LNER' on the tender was abbreviated to 'NE'. *PC/Colour-Rail (NE119)*

Above:
Class B17/2 No 2833 *Kimbolton Castle* bounds along near Brookmans Park with an up express in 1937. Action colour this early is hard to find.
K. H. Leech/Colour-Rail (NE61)

football clubs whose grounds lay in LNER territory, but there was a little stretching of the point in one or two cases. Two engines (Nos 2859 and 2839) carried the name *Norwich City*, but *Ipswich Town* was (somewhat surprisingly) never used. These engines carried a cast half-football beneath the nameplates, and the splasher was decorated with the club's colours. The two 'B17/5s' were renamed *East Anglian* (No 2859) and *City of London* (No 2870) to designate their connection with the 'East Anglian'.

Above:
This is the only known colour picture of a streamlined Class B17/5, taken at Liverpool Street Yard shortly after Nationalisation.
No 61659 *East Anglian* is clearly in unlined black livery, but on page 67 the same locomotive is portrayed in lined green livery of some shade, so at some time after its acquisition by British Railways a repaint took place — and not for the better.
On the road beside the 'B17/5' stands Norwich-based Class B1 No 1047, still in full LNER livery — but take careful note of where the shed allocation appears on the buffer-beam. *R. E. Vincent*

Below:
Class B17/1 No 61623 *Lambton Castle* heads northwards at Potters Bar with a Cambridge train of Gresley stock in Coronation Year (1953). This is almost the classic British Railways picture — engine in Brunswick green with the original totem and the stock in carmine and cream.
E. Oldham/Colour-Rail (BRE108)

Above:
The date is 25 January 1936 and No 2847 *Helmingham Hall* has charge of the 12.5pm Wolferton – King's Cross at Potters Bar. This is a very sad duty, for the working is the funeral train of His Late Majesty King George V. At the time, No 2847 was the newest 'B17' in traffic and inherited the duty because No 2800 *Sandringham* (which, for obvious reasons, would have performed the duty) was laid off with boiler trouble. Note the Royal Headcode of four lamps. *Ken Nunn collection/LCGB*

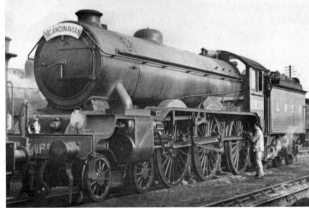

Above:
No 2836 *Harlaxton Manor* on shed with LNER-style 'Scandinavian' headboard. *Photomatic (Wholesale) Ltd*

Right:
In 1937 the directors of the LNER decided that the streamline era should come to East Anglia, and two members of the 'B17' class were chosen to be streamlined in the style of the 'A4' Pacifics, for hauling a new London–Norwich prestige train to be known as the 'East Anglian'. The engines chosen were Nos 2859 and 2870, and these were reclassified 'B17/5'. The former carried no fewer than five sets of nameplates during its life: originally named *Norwich City*, it bore curved plates with the half-football before having a straight set fitted when streamlined on 13 September 1937; for just one day (believed 20 September) it carried a straight set with the legend *City of Norwich* before a straight *East Anglian* set appeared, and, finally, when the engine was de-streamlined, it was fitted with a curved set which it retained until withdrawn from service. The locomotive is seen here near Ipswich with an up 'East Anglian' working, but the date is lost. The lining on the apple green is clearly discernible.
Photomatic (Wholesale) Ltd

Left:
No 2870 *City of London* at speed near Ipswich with an express for the capital — fully streamlined and a beautiful sight in apple green.
Photomatic (Wholesale) Ltd

Above:
The official photograph of the 'East Anglian', with No 2859 at its head.
Real Photographs

Above:
Class B17/6 No 61663 *Everton* at Great Shelford in May 1958, presenting the opportunity for this wonderful shot looking down into the cab. This is an excellent picture, as the colours of the nameplate and the half-football stand out well on the splasher and the cab lining is clearly shown. And note the fire-glow.
D. M. C. Hepburne-Scott/Colour-Rail (BRE364)

Above:
This picture dates from April 1948 and shows that ideas on the new liveries to be adopted by British Railways were being formulated quite early on. A number of locomotives from the constituent companies Nationalised on 1 January 1948 were exhibited at Marylebone for inspection. Class B17/6 No 61661 *Sheffield Wednesday* was finished in apple green lined in black and white — very similar to LNER passenger-locomotive livery — with 'BRITISH RAILWAYS' upon the tender; a front number-plate was fitted and the cabside numbers were hand-painted. *DOW/Colour-Rail (BRE1006)*

Liveries

Being express-passenger locomotives the 'B17s' were painted
by the LNER in lined apple green and, upon passing into BR
ownership, all received lined Brunswick green. From November
1941, in accordance with LNER policy, plain unlined black was
applied, and from 1942 only 'NE' was displayed upon the
tenders, and the club colours on the splashers were painted out.
Mention must be made of the treatment of the two streamlined
examples: upon streamlining, both received apple green, with
the wheel fairings in black; during the war, both were painted
black, but in July 1949 when a Diagram 100A boiler was fitted,
No 61659 was repainted in apple green with 'BRITISH
RAILWAYS' in full upon the tender, and it received a smokebox
numberplate. No 61670 was never repainted green whilst
streamlined and continued to run in unlined black, but from
August 1948 with 'BRITISH RAILWAYS' on the tender.

Above:
The date of this photograph is lost, but it serves to illustrate the early treatment of the 'B17' class post-Nationalisation: No 61622 *Alnwick Castle* is in Brunswick green with 'BRITISH RAILWAYS' upon the tender.
Real Photographs

Above right:
Sadly the only known colour picture of a 'B17/5' shows *East Anglian* in British Railways black livery. However, this picture is irrefutable proof that, for some time at least, the locomotive ran post-Nationalisation in green. On 30 July 1949 No 61659 was stopped at signals outside Colchester station with a Liverpool Street–Norwich express; the green stops at the first boiler-band and the black is brought down in a vertical line, the number being carried in signwriting upon the buffer beam and 'BRITISH RAILWAYS' upon the tender — in all likelihood the colour is LNER apple green, as the locomotive is believed to have been repainted thus in July 1949. The valances over the driving wheels were removed to simplify wartime maintenance and were never replaced. *R. C. Riley*

Right:
Sister locomotive *City of London* in repose at Norwich shed as British Railways No 61670 on Sunday 24 July 1949, apparently in black livery.
Roger Harrison

Right:
Class B17/6 No 61649 *Sheffield United* lifts a local out of Woodbridge in September 1957. The train is in carmine and cream, but by now it is BR Mk 1 stock. *PGL/Colour-Rail (BRE1199)*

Below right:
The condition in which most people will now remember the 'B17s' — in British Railways Brunswick green livery. This picture of No 61612 *Houghton Hall* was taken at Norwich shed in July 1959 and shows the engine looking somewhat unkempt, for there is little evidence of lining and it is rather dirty. In reality there was little outward difference between the 'B17' sub-classes which had the GER-pattern tender, with the exception of the Westinghouse pump. *Photomatic (Wholesale) Ltd*

Above:
Class B17/6 No 61652 *Darlington* heads south from Cambridge towards the end of its life; the locomotive was withdrawn in September 1959. Close examination of the nameplate reveals that, as with other locomotives named after football teams, this incorporated the relevant team colours — in Darlington's case, black and white. Appropriately, this locomotive was built at Darlington, in April 1936, and was converted to 'B17/6' in March 1948 — one of the first to be so treated.
Derek Penney

Right:
This three-quarter left rear view of No 61652 *Darlington* at Cambridge shed in July 1959 illustrates well the manner in which the application of the relevant football club's colours was treated on the centre splasher. During the war, when the locomotives were finished in unlined black with 'NE' upon the tender, the various clubs' colours were painted over, but these were soon restored with the coming of peace. Whilst the 'B17/4s' were originally intended for working on former Great Central lines, they tended to gravitate to East Anglia as the Great Eastern turntables were replaced. *Photomatic (Wholesale) Ltd*

Below right:
Melton Hall was built as a 'B17/4' and delivered to traffic at Norwich in April 1933 numbered 2838. August 1946 saw the change of number to 1638, and the British Railways number was applied exactly two years later, with rebuilding to 'B17/6' taking place in December 1948. As No 61638 the engine is seen leaving Norwich with a Yarmouth train on 2 September 1951 at the head of a rake of Southern stock.
Philip J. Kelley

Left:
The scene at Yarmouth South Town shed on 22 February 1959, with a 'B1' and a 'B17' receiving attention; Nos 61311 and 61670 *City of London* (the latter long since de-streamlined) both have their smokebox doors open, and the centre and left-hand cylinders of the 'B17' have their covers removed. The general clutter of a working steam shed is well illustrated. *Philip J. Kelley*

Above:
The final 'B17', No 61672 *West Ham United*, crosses Trowse swing-bridge at Norwich on Sunday 4 April 1959. *Roger Harrison*

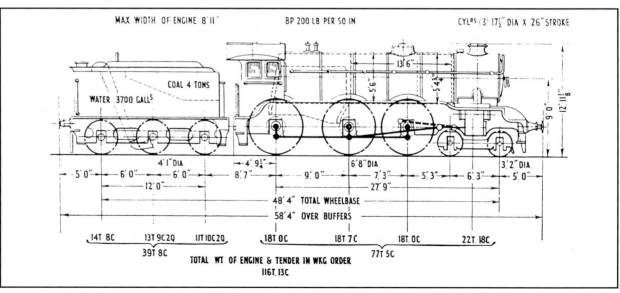

MAX WIDTH OF ENGINE 8'11"   BP 200 LB PER SQ IN   CYL^{RS} (3) 17½" DIA X 26" STROKE

COAL 4 TONS

WATER 3700 GALL^S

13' 6"

5' 6"   5' 4¾"

9' 0"

12' 11⅛"

4' 1" DIA.

5' 0"   6' 0"   6' 0"   8' 7"   9' 0"   7' 3"   5' 3"   6' 3"   5' 0"

12' 0"   4' 9½"   6' 8" DIA.   3' 2" DIA.

27' 9"

48' 4" TOTAL WHEELBASE

58' 4" OVER BUFFERS

14T 8C   13T 9C 2Q   11T 10C 2Q   18T 0C   18T 7C   18T 0C   22T 18C

39T 8C   77T 5C

TOTAL WT OF ENGINE & TENDER IN WKG ORDER

116T 13C

Thompson Class B1
6ft 2in engines

This was without question the most numerous class of LNER locomotives, for a total of 410 was built by the LNER and British Railways, though only 409 were ever in traffic together following an accident at Rivenhall End on 7 March 1950 which destroyed No 61057. Sir Nigel Gresley died in harness in 1941 and was succeeded to the position of Chief Mechanical Engineer by his deputy Edward Thompson, who swiftly instituted a programme of standardisation. The remit for his new 4-6-0 (which was to be designated "just Class B", to quote Thompson's own words) was to replace all 4-6-0s "not covered by the 6ft 2in Pacifics, 'D11s', 'D49s' and all heavy 4-4-0

engines, 'C1s' and other passenger Atlantics, 'K2s', 'K3s', 'J39s' and 'J6s' and other 0-6-0s at present subject to fairly high speeds".

The first example of the new engine emerged from Darlington in December 1942, classified 'B1' (the existing ex-GCR 'B1s' being reclassified as 'B18s'). In keeping with Thompson's views on simplicity and standardisation, it had two outside 20x26in cylinders, Walschaerts motion with 10in piston valves, straight footplating, boiler pressed to 225lb/sq in and a 4,200gal Group Standard tender. Tractive effort was 26,878lb, and the design weighed 123 tons 3cwt. Some later examples were equipped with ex-'C9' 4,125gal NER tenders and weighed 117 tons 15cwt. The first 40 were built at Darlington between December 1942 and December 1947; the original 10 were ordered in August 1942 and the remaining 30

in May 1944. North British erected 100 between April 1946 and April 1947 under Order No L958 placed in August 1945, with a further 50 coming from Vulcan Foundry between April and August 1947 under Order No 2333 placed in January 1946. That same month, North British received order No L963, which called for 150 examples, and these were delivered between May 1947 and September 1948. Between November 1948 and July 1949 British Railways Gorton built 10 which had been ordered in December 1947, while Darlington built 10 from July to October 1949 that had been ordered in November 1947. Somewhat surprisingly, North British received an order for 40 in September 1948, but delivery did not commence until March 1949, with the last one being delivered in April 1952. In February 1949 the final batch of 10 was ordered from Darlington, and these were delivered into traffic between March and June 1950. Production of the 410 locomotives had thus been spread over 10 years, through war into peace and for two operating companies. Virtually no rebuilding took place, and the 'B1' fulfilled its remit as a standard engine, being found the length and breadth of the LNER system; in BR days it was even seen in Great Western territory and on the Southern Region.

Numbering and Naming
The initial Darlington-built batch of 'B1s' was numbered from 8301 to 8310, which required the renumbering of six 'F7' 2-4-2Ts. The comprehensive 1943 renumbering of LNER locomotives saw the existing 'B1s' allocated numbers 1000-9; at the time, 330 more were on order (see above), allocated 1010-1339, and further renumbering of other classes was necessary as production of 'B1s' continued. At Nationalisation 274 of Thompson's 4-6-0s passed to British Railways, which added 60,000 to their numbers and continued the series as fresh examples emerged from works,

after a brief period in 1948 when Nos 1288-1303 appeared with an 'E' prefix.

Of the 410 'B1s' built, just 59 were named — the first 41 after antelopes and a further 17 after directors of the LNER. No 8306 was named *Bongo*, and it was as '*Bongos*' that enthusiasts knew the class. Given the number of species of antelope which inhabit our planet it is surprising that those responsible for the naming these engines managed to duplicate two of the names, as *Nyala* /*Inyala* and *Wildebeeste*/*Gnu* (one of the shortest names ever applied to a British locomotive) are, respectively, two names for the same animal. Yet only one was named after a British deer. The only 'B1' to receive a name after Nationalisation was No 61379, which in 1951 was named *Mayflower* and in 1952 had plaques fitted to the cabsides which read: 'This locomotive was named Mayflower 13th July 1951 as a symbol of the ties between the two towns of Boston and of the lasting friendship between the U.S.A. and the British Commonwealth'.

Liveries

Appearing in wartime, the first 10 'B1s' were painted in unlined black livery with 'NE' upon the tenders, but before Nationalisation this was extended to 'LNER', and three acquired apple green with black and white lining. The first was No 8304 in September 1945 for Royal Train duties from Cambridge, albeit still with 'NE' on the tender; in January 1946 the number was changed to 1003 and 'LNER' applied to the tender. In September 1947 the same treatment was given to No 1000, and No 61002 was similarly painted at Cowlairs but with 'BRITISH RAILWAYS' on the tender. Nos 1010-39, meanwhile, appeared new in apple green, but North British turned out Nos 1040-93 in LNER lined black, apple green making an appearance on NBL products only from No 1094. Following Nationalisation, locomotives from No E1288 were delivered with 'BRITISH RAILWAYS' on the tender, in place of 'LNER'. British Railways duly decided that mixed-traffic locomotives should be painted black, lined with grey, red and straw, and this livery made its appearance from No 61340. Shortly afterwards, the 'BRITISH RAILWAYS' tender lettering was superseded by the first style of lion-and-wheel emblem, and, over time, most 'B1s' carried both styles of BR tender emblem.

Left:
Just three years and four months later, on 6 August 1949 *Roedeer* is seen at Norwich shed, having acquired its British Railways number (61040) and wearing British Railways mixed-traffic livery of lined black, with the ownership spelt out in full on the tender.
Roger Harrison

Above:
Two 'B1s', No 1182 nearer the camera in apple green and No 1071 further away in LNER black, are captured alongside an unidentified Stanier Class 5 4-6-0 of the LMS. Although the location is unknown, and this particular photograph is undated, it can be approximately dated to between July 1947 (when No 1182 was built at the Vulcan Foundry) and April 1948 (when No 1071 received its BR number). No 1071 was a North British-built example of the class, dating from August 1946. *Ian Allan Library via C. N. Weston*

Above:
An almost perfect study of a 'B1' in apple green at its best. No 1134 stands with polished rods at Elgin in 1948.
J. M. Jarvis/Colour-Rail (NE33)

Right:
'B1' No 1268 waits to depart Wakefield Westgate with a down stopping passenger train in 1948. This is slightly work-stained apple green and gives a good impression of the treatment which the LNER meted out to the driving wheels of its passenger locomotives. Built in December 1947 by North British, No 1268 was one of the last of the class to be delivered to the LNER prior to Nationalisation and had therefore been in service only a matter of months when this photograph was taken. *H. M. Lane/Colour-Rail (NE162)*

Right:
On Guy Fawkes Day 1948 North British-built 'B1' No 61318 waits to depart Birmingham New Street. The engine still carries fully-lined LNER apple green but is adorned with its British Railways number and lettering. Until an emblem was decided upon the post-Nationalisation ownership was indicated in this manner. *T. J. Edgington*

Below right:
Same station, same pose on 26 April 1949: the cabside numbering of black-liveried No 61202 is somewhat smaller than on No 61318, the latter's being the size finally decided upon.
T. J. Edgington

Left:
Following Nationalisation and before the locomotive numbering scheme to be used by British Railways had been decided upon, the numbers of the engines of the four railway companies were prefixed with a letter commensurate with the company to which they formerly belonged. Ex-LNER locomotives were prefixed 'E', and on 9 April 1949 'B1' 4-6-0 No E1300 is seen at the head of the 2pm King's Cross – Cambridge Class B semi-fast in the cutting north of Potters Bar. The engine retains apple-green livery but the tender is lettered 'BRITISH RAILWAYS'; the train consists entirely of Gresley stock still in teak livery. *E. D. Bruton*

Lower left:
It is surprising that, three years after Nationalisation, a 'B1' should still retain LNER apple-green livery with 'BRITISH RAILWAYS' upon the tender, but on Thursday 23 August 1951 No 61134 was photographed so adorned at Keith, heading a train of Gresley stock in carmine and cream livery.
Roger Harrison

Above:
Just by way of proving how far the 'B1s' roved, in September 1962 No 61039 *Steinbok* had found its way onto the Western Region and was in alien surroundings at Swindon shed — a long way from its Northampton home. The locomotive wears the later BR emblem upon the tender and is in somewhat work-stained condition. *J. G. Dewing/Colour-Rail (BRW983)*

Above:
No 61032 *Stembok* (with the later British Railways emblem on the tender) crosses the maze of trackwork at the north end of York station on Sunday 11 July 1964. Note the clerestory-roofed coach. *Roger Harrison*

Left:
Heading a train of maroon-liveried Gresley stock and coupled to a self-weighing tender, No 61095 departs Norwich on Monday 6 June 1960.
Roger Harrison

Right:
Upon withdrawal from service a number of 'B1s' were transferred to Departmental Stock for use as heating boilers; one such was No 61252, which was transferred as No 22 in November 1963 and finally withdrawn in May 1964. It is seen at Ipswich with its new number and outwardly in good condition. *H. N. James*

Right:
From August 1964 at Annesley shed comes this picture of Class B1 *William Henton Carver* in simply appalling condition. The cab-side number claims that it is No 1215, but by this time in its life the locomotive had become No 61215, and there is a front number-plate to prove it.
B. Henderson collection/ Colour-Rail (BRE1332)

Below right:
No 61263 is seen at speed in the late 1950s, carrying the later BR emblem on its tender. It is hauling a mixed rake of Gresley and early BR standard coaches, two of the latter carrying the carmine and cream livery.
Ian Allan Library via C. N. Weston

Right:
No 61076 runs light-engine towards Haymarket station during October 1961. 'B1' and 'HAYMARKET' can be clearly seen on the buffer-beam, and, with the coming of electrification, signs warning of the overhead power lines have been mounted on the forward-facing edges of the running-plate. *George M. Staddon/ Colour-Rail (SC1010)*

Right:
On 7 June 1959 'B1'
No 61249 passes through
Mistley station with the
down 'Scandinavian'
(3.5pm Liverpool Street–
Harwich Parkeston Quay).
The stock is a mixture of
Gresley and Thompson in
maroon livery. Note the
condition of the station's
gardens! *A. R. J. Frost*

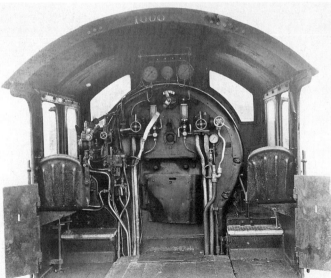

Left:
The inside of the cab of 'B1' No 1000 *Springbok*, photographed in 1947.
National Railway Museum

Left:
It is 24 March 1951, and 'B1' No 61363 passes through Manningtree on its way to Harwich Parkeston Quay with the down 'Day Continental' having left Liverpool Street at 9.25am.
The headboard (which bears British and Dutch flags) is carried on the high top lamp-iron of the smokebox. *H. N. James*

Left:
It is 24 March 1951, and 'B1' No 61363 passes through Manningtree on its way to Harwich Parkeston Quay with the down 'Day Continental' having left Liverpool Street at 9.25am.
The headboard (which bears British and Dutch flags) is carried on the high top lamp-iron of the smokebox. *H. N. James*

Left:
Thompson LNER Class B1.

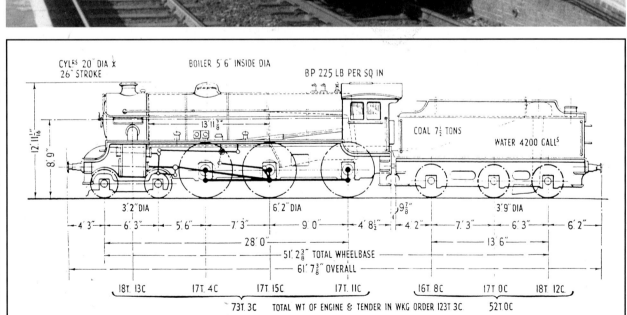

CYL^RS 20" DIA x 26" STROKE
BOILER 5' 6" INSIDE DIA
B P 225 LB PER SQ IN
COAL 7½ TONS
WATER 4200 GALL^S
12' 11 11/16"
8' 9"
13' 11 3/8"
3' 2" DIA
6' 2" DIA
9 7/8"
3' 9" DIA
4' 3" — 6' 3" — 5' 6" — 7' 3" — 9' 0" — 4' 8½" — 4' 2" — 7' 3" — 6' 3" — 6' 2"
28' 0"
13' 6"
51' 2 3/8" TOTAL WHEELBASE
61' 7 3/8" OVERALL
18T. 13C   17T. 4C   17T. 15C   17T. 11C   16T. 8C   17T. 0C   18T. 12C
73T. 3C   TOTAL WT OF ENGINE & TENDER IN WKG ORDER 123T 3C   52T. 0C

Thompson Class B2 — Rebuilds of Gresley Class B17 6ft 8in engines

Thompson's 'B2' was, for all practical purposes, a 'B1' with 6in-larger driving wheels. Originally 20 conversions of 'B17s' to 'B2s' were authorised, and an initial order for 10 was placed in October 1944. On 2 November No 2871 *Manchester City* entered Darlington Works following an incident at Colchester when it broke its centre connecting rod; by the middle of the month it had been earmarked as the first rebuild, but it did not re-enter traffic until August of the following year. Being one of the final batch of 'B17s', it was coupled to a Group Standard tender and was the only 'B2' to be so equipped,

notwithstanding the initial intention that they should all have Group Standard tenders. In February 1946 No 2871 became No 1671, and in April the name was changed to *Royal Sovereign* when it received the honour of becoming the official Royal Engine and the accolade of the Stratford mark of a white cab roof. Under the rebuild, gone were the graceful curves of the Gresley running-plate, to be replaced with straight lines; boiler pressure was raised to 225lb/sq in and tractive effort slightly reduced to 24,863lb, and the locomotive weighed 125½ tons. Eight more rebuilds were carried out by the LNER and one by British Railways, thus fulfilling the order for 10; the locomotives selected had their original GER-pattern tenders replaced by redundant tenders from withdrawn 'C7s' and 'P1s'. With the ex-NER tenders they weighed 117 tons 12cwt and with the 'P1' tenders 112 tons 18cwt.

Above:
'B17/1' No 2803 *Framlingham* was rebuilt in October 1946, receiving its new number (1603) at the same time; during rebuilding, the Westinghouse pump was removed and the GER-pattern tender was replaced with tender No 8663 from a withdrawn ex-NER Class C7 Atlantic. The 'B2s' were painted apple green by the LNER and Brunswick green by British Railways; they were classified by the latter as passenger locomotives, whereas the 'B1s' were regarded as mixed-traffic engines. *Photomatic (Wholesale) Ltd*

Above:
No 61632 *Belvoir Castle* was rebuilt from Class B17/2 in July 1946 and was coupled to tender 5294 from condemned Class P1 2-8-2 No 2394 and is seen here carrying Colchester shed code at Stratford shed in October 1953. Upon the withdrawal of No 61671, this engine was renamed *Royal Sovereign* and became the Stratford Royal Engine in October 1958, but the honour was short-lived, as withdrawal came in February 1959. *LGRP/David & Charles*

Right:
No 1607 *Blickling* was the last-but-one 'B2' rebuild, in May 1947; it retained the Westinghouse pump and was coupled to ex-NER Class C7 tender No 8636. Note the difference in the coal rail between this locomotive and No 1603 in the previous picture. *Photomatic (Wholesale) Ltd*

Numbering

The 'B2s' were numbered in sequence with their original 'B17' numbering.

Liveries

The nine 'B2s' rebuilt by the LNER were all painted in unlined black with 'NE' upon the tender, but No 2815 later appeared with 'LNER' instead. When No 2871/1671 was allocated to Royal Train duties it was repainted in apple green but with 'BRITISH RAILWAYS' on the tender. The rest remained in unlined black until No 61603 was painted apple green at Stratford with its new ownership lettered on the tender, and No 61644 emerged rebuilt from Darlington similarly painted. In October 1949 Stratford outshopped No 61617 in apple green with the BR emblem on the tender and with green-painted cylinder casings. As express-passenger engines, all were eventually painted in BR Brunswick green with black/orange lining.

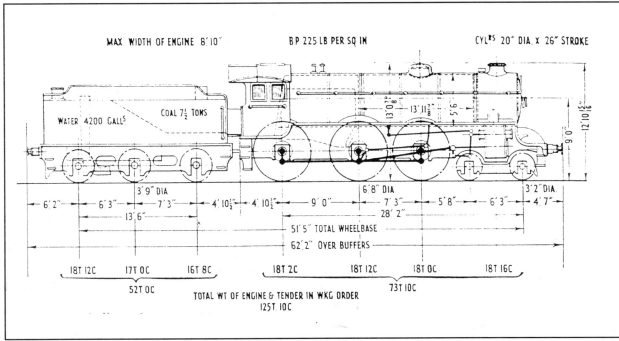

Right:
At the close of the 20th century it was still possible to see two LNER 4-6-0s in steam together. On Sunday 8 February 1998 'B12' No 8572 and 'B1' No 1264 arrived at Leicester North at the head of the 9.30am Loughborough–Leicester North service on the Great Central Railway. They made a glorious sight, both decked out in fully lined apple-green livery; teak stock would have perfected the scene, but we must be grateful for what the preservation movement has saved for us. *Roger Harrison*

Left:
During 1999 the 'B12' was repainted in BR mixed-traffic livery of black lined in red, grey and straw, with the later BR totem on the tender. On Sunday 21 November 1999 it was photographed near the signalbox in Sheringham Yard at its home on the North Norfolk Railway; 32A (on the smokebox) was the code for Norwich shed, from whence it was withdrawn in 1961, having been the last 'B12' in traffic. *Roger Harrison*

IN PRESERVATION